Staffords Hauliers Two

This John Heath photo was taken at Shirley's depot in 2012. L-R: Bill Crombie, Clayton King, Aaron King, Axl King, Arthur Shirley, Chris Sheldon, Chris Woolliscroft, Stanley Salt.

Ros Unwin

Front Cover: Vince Cooke in his Kendrick eight-wheeler. Vince drove this from new for about 18 months before he went on to artics. 1968 *David Bloor Collection*

CHURNET VALLEY BOOKS
1 King Street, Leek, Staffordshire. ST13 5NW 01538 399033 www.leekbooks.co.uk
© Ros Unwin and Churnet Valley Books 2013
ISBN 9781904546849

George Deakin with ex-Wincanton ERF. *George Deakin Collection*

This Chris Smith photo was taken at the NEC in 2009. Stan had to be persuaded to pose for it.
Stan was Haulier of the Year in 1999.

CONTENTS

Maurice Hill's Foden with Gardner LXB 180 taken at Gateshead in August 1968

Maurice Hill Collection.

Gordon Barker (Woof Woof) was the driver here in front of Walsall Power Station.
David Bloor Collection

Foden 8 wheeler with Gardner LX. Most of the bodies were by Edbro. This has a tilt cab; the drivers called these 'pneumonia cabs' because the rubber seal where they tilted used to perish making the cabs draughty. Drivers would stuff newspapers or rags in the gap causing many a fire!

David Bloor Collection

HORACE KENDRICK LIMITED - Bill Kendrick

The Kendrick family haulage business started in Walsall in 1860. In 1908 my grandfather, Horace, decided to set up on his own, operating on land in Mary Street, Walsall, with twenty horse drawn vehicles and some light motor vehicles. In the 1950s he moved to a new yard in Green Lane from where the business continued to trade until we closed down in 1986. In the early days we ran Atkinsons and Albions but in 1953 we purchased our first Foden.

In the beginning... This picture is of Bill's great grandfather on the right in the foreground with his son, Horace, founder of Horace Kendrick Ltd, standing by the wheel. *Bill Kendrick Collection*

When my grandfather died the business was taken over by my dad, Bill Snr and his brother, Horace Snr. I can remember going with my dad to the depot during the school holidays. Some mornings he'd be driving along in his Jaguar with me in the passenger seat when he'd spot one of our vehicles going the other way and he'd flash the driver to stop. When he'd pulled over he'd tell me to climb in the cab and spend the day with the driver on the lorry.

As well as haulage business we had a petrol station and I'd work on the pumps when I was young. We also sold cars for a period in the 60s and 70s; we were agents for Simca but relinquished the franchise and converted the showroom into larger offices. Edna Reece, a very efficient lady who had been with the company from the 1940s, was in charge of the office staff. We had quite a few characters working for us including Jack Booker who lived in Cross Street and was very popular. Then there was George Cotterill and Vince Cooke who were good, conscientious workers. The men used to get £2.50 for a night's subsistence which was supposed to be for their lodging and breakfast but most of them spent the night in the cab and used the money for other things. It was cold in those old Mickey Mouse cabs (not sleepers) and they'd wake up like a piece of ice. They worked hard!

When I went into the business properly in 1969 at 21, I worked in the Traffic Office under Tom Faulkner and Doug Taylor who taught me the job; they had both started with the company when they came back from the war. Doug died quite young which left Tom and me doing the traffic. My cousin, Horace ran the maintenance side of the business. We had a very good foreman in the garage, Eric Smith who lived in one of the two company houses at the yard (my grandmother lived in the other) but unfortunately while working on a lorry one day he suffered

A Chinese Six, 28 tonner, Maurice Hill's again but before the accident at Brecon; a couple of kinks on the body can just be seen. The first artic they had was actually LDH 712D that Maurice also drove. Jack Booker was to have the second one but didn't like it so he went on to a 26 tonner and Norman Hillyard had it.   *David Bloor Collection.*

a brain haemorrhage and died. It was very traumatic. He was greatly missed.

Sometimes I had to go to Fodens in the Transit to get spares. It was always an experience because Fodens at Sandbach was like a town; it was massive. Anyone going there to get parts was given a voucher to go to the canteen and have lunch: pie, chips and beans and a big pint mug of tea. You'd get a pudding as well, probably apple crumble or spotted dick and custard.

There were four directors of our company: Bill Snr, Horace Snr, Horace Jnr and myself. The business was very successful during the 1960s; we were running over seventy vehicles. However, like most companies at the time, we had problems with the unions. This was especially so during the miners' strikes when flying pickets would blockade the premises. Obviously, we worked during the strikes but it was very difficult because all the pits were being picketed; it was very dangerous for the drivers.

By 1986 a lot of the pits were closing and the foundries changed over to electric so foundry coke, which was a big part of our business, wasn't required. This, along with EEC regulations and the advent of the tachograph led us to the decision to close the business and invest in something new. My father was a very good friend of Harry Whitehouse (known as 'The Bingo King') who had brought Bingo from London to the Midlands. Harry was very influential in the bingo world and we decided to invest - the business grew and was very successful. We formed a company called Newtown Entertainments which we eventually sold to Ladbrokes. Later, we formed another company, Jarglen which we sold to Gala in 1999.

This photo taken in 1968 shows some of the Kendrick fleet. L-R the wrecker, three 8 wheel tilt cabs, an 8 wheeler which was one of the first 26ton gross vehicles, the oldest vehicle - a 24 tonner, and finally a 1968 semi tilt cab which was Vince Cooke's outfit. *Bill Kendrick Collection*

The Wrecker was Jack Booker's old vehicle. *David Bloor Collection.*

LEFT:
Bill's grandfather, Horace, the founder of the company. Bill Kendrick Collection

Bill's parents, Bill Sr and Win, enjoying a day at the races. Early 1960s. *Bill Kendrick Collection.*

Bill in 1976. *Bill Kendrick Collection*

Bill's Uncle Horace (Horace Sr) with Foden representative, J Nicholls. *David Bloor Collection.*

Vince Cooke

When I started in transport I was driving a digger for old Tommy Blakemore at the old Anglesey Siding which is where Charrington's Oil Tanks is now on the A5. They used to bring the coal from the collieries by train down to the siding and throw it on the trucks. I wanted to get on the road and a guy named Vin Shelley wanted a driver for a petrol Dodge. This was in 1955. I went from there to Winfields - bigger motors, more money. We used to get two shillings a ton to chuck coal on which was DS (double screened) or slack. You got 10 tons a time on so if you did three a day you made £3 a day and that was big money in those days. There was a machine with a grab on but if you used that you only got 1/6 so we chucked it on for the extra! It was hard work; you used to have to shave the skin on the pads of your hands every week because of the calluses.

I stayed on the tippers when I went to Kendricks at Walsall. In those days when the money dropped you went. Then I went to Robin Taylor at Lichfield. I'd been waiting for a job at Jones's but you had to wait for someone to retire or die. I'd only been at Taylors a month and this job came up. Fortunately Robin was on holiday when I left.

At Kendricks we only had one trailer each and your number plate was bolted to it. You never dropped a trailer. So if you came in from Durham with a load of coke at Elkingtons and they hadn't got room for it, you had to park up until the next day unless there was someone off and there was a spare motor. Kendricks were big; they ran over 70 Fodens.

One of the people I remember from those days was Gordon Barker a good bloke and a great driver. They used to call him Woof. Everyone had a nickname; I was Cookie or Curly because I had curly hair then. Another driver was Jackie Booker. Jackie had worked for Kendricks when they still had one or two horses. He lived round the corner from the yard.

I remember an occasion when I had a diff go on my vehicle; all Kendrick vehicles were single drive, they never had doubles. Anyway, this vehicle was surging and Eric Smith who was in charge of the garage told me 'the diff's on the way out but it'll be alright.' So I went to Avenue Coke Works at Chesterfield, came off the weighbridge and went up to the canteen for breakfast. When I got back and climbed in the vehicle she wouldn't go, so I rang in again. Tommy Faulkner said, 'Come on down, I'll get you a ride home and you can come back in the morning with Jackie Booker.' Jackie was on an eight wheeler tipping at Sheffield, loading at Avenue at that time. So we went up, put the bar on and Jackie brought me back. Mine was 24 ton and I never felt Jack change gear all the way to Walsall. Not once. It was as if it was automatic. Brilliant. What a driver!

I loved the Foden 12 speed gearbox; it was something else! You were part of it. Four on the floor and three on the column - high, direct and low. Split shifts every time. This was way before the Volvos and Scanias.

I remember being with Jim Boot at Kendricks and we were both coming up from South Wales and pulled in at the Old Yat Café. At that time Kendricks had 73 or 74 vehicles. This Welshman pulls on with a horsebox. He comes in and can see that we're Kendrick drivers and starts to talk about how many Kendrick lorries there were on the road and says, 'No matter where you go you see Kendricks. I was down Brighton yesterday and saw one. How many have you got?' Jim had a very dry sense of humour and quick as anything and dead serious says 'There's him with the artic and there's me... well, there's seven of us altogether.' The man says, 'God, they must fly!'

Teddy Steadman was another character. He came off the weighbridge at Bedwas Coke Ovens one day. It was a very awkward place; you went up a side road and the weighbridge was at the side of the road and there was a bit of a step. So he got on there, got loaded and came off. He changed up twice and ended up upside down in somebody's garden. They had to get Wynn's out to put it back on its feet. I was in the yard when Ted came in and Horace (Kendrick) says, 'Ed, how did you manage that?' Ted looked at him and said 'Dead easy!'

Maurice Hill

I went to Kendricks in March 1966 and was given an eight wheeler. This didn't have coke boards so I did all the low access jobs. In the following December we had the first artic and they called me to the office and told me I'd be driving it. I said, 'I've only been here a few months; there are plenty of guys here with longer service'. But I was told that Mr Bill and Mr Horace had decided I was to have it. It was a four wheel tractor, tandem trailer, 30 ton gross Foden with a 150 Gardner engine. When they put the weight up to 32 ton we had to have five axles so then we had two twin steers and two tri-axle trailers. The two tri-axle trailers went on to the two four wheel tractors and the tandem trailers went on the six wheel units which had Gardner LXBs in.

I remember an occasion when a lad from the bank wanted to go along with one of the drivers for a week to see what it was like and I was told I'd be taking him. I told him we'd be setting of at 4.00 am and if he came at five past I'd be gone and sure enough, he was there early. So off we go that first day to Gateshead and we were tipping nice, easy stuff that was like gravel. After we'd tipped we had to go down to Lake and Elliot, the people who make the hydraulic jacks, to get loaded from the tip. They had this RB21 with a dragline loading these great big lumps (1 to 2 tons apiece) which were the runnings from the

Maurice Hill at Gateshead in 1968 RDH 955F. This was an experimental trailer; it was the first all-welded aluminium body they did. *Maurice Hill Collection*

bottom of the furnaces. So this RB was picking them up and putting them in the body. The ground was horrendous and obviously the vehicle couldn't get out without help so they attached the RB line to the towing hitch on the front of the wagon with the Cat D9 positioned at the back of it and we got out with the RB pulling us and the D9 pushing from behind.

A week or two later the guy from the bank brought some photos in to show me. I was standing by the office window looking at them and one of these was a snap of what had happened at the tip. Mr Bill came out and was looking at them and when he saw this particular picture he asked me where it was taken. I said 'That's down the tip at Lake and Elliots, Braintree.' 'Who the bloody hell sent you there?' So I told him and this bloke was sitting at the desk next to him. Mr Bill wasn't best pleased 'Don't ever send one of my trucks anywhere like that again!' I could see his point because that wagon would be worth about £6000 which was a lot of money then. It was a nice truck.

We had a guy named Kenny Morris who was a quiet but very pleasant man. When he was at work he was a good worker and a really steady guy. His mum and dad kept a little pub on the main road at the back of Brownhills called the Chase Inn and he used to go up there at weekends and help out, but after a while he started to duck work on Mondays. Anyway, one day he'd just gone to the office to put his papers in with what he'd done for the day and was walking away when a voice said 'Aah, Mr Morris....' It was Bill Kendrick '...what's this four day a week business?' Quick as anything Ken said 'I'm very sorry, Mr Bill, but I can't manage on three!' and carried on out through the door. He didn't get the sack or anything because he was a good worker.

Vince Cooke, Norman Hillyard, Teddy Steadman, Old Cliff Bowen, Johnny Hardiman were some of the people I remember at Kendricks. The foreman in the garage was Eric Smith who lived next door to Mrs Kendrick, the wife of old Horace and there were a couple of guys working for him named Les Slymn and his brother-in-law, Sid Bishop. Later, Les and Sid both went to work for S Jones where Les was Foreman Fitter and Sid was Fleet Engineer. I also remember Johnny Plant and his father, Albert 'Quacker' Plant, Ernie Hathaway and Jack Booker whose old motor I'd had when I started 316 UDH.

I left the company in 1970 when I had an accident; it was the second one I had in RDH 955F The first one was when I turned it over in Brecon when I was going down to Llanelli with a load of foundry sand in. I went down a grass verge and went over, virtually upside down. I managed to crawl out of the windscreen and went to find a phone. I rang the depot and they came out and dragged it out. It went back to Fodens to be repaired. The second accident happened when I was coming up from the other side of Exeter. It was in the morning coming round Bridgwater where the steel works was. There was a low loader in front and a few of us were queuing behind on this dual carriageway. Anyway, a guy in front hit the verge and slammed his brakes on and everybody piled in. I hit the bloke in front which was a Whitbread Brewery wagon and, of course, did some damage on the radiator so it was a tow job. The man who'd run in the back of me was driving an Austin Cambridge car. We were all sitting there when the police turned up. When the policeman came over and asked what had happened I said 'It's him in the Austin Cambridge; he pushed us all forward!' He wasn't amused.

Maurice Hill at Lake and Elliotts, Braintree in August 1968 where his vehicle had to be pulled by the RB and pushed from behind by the D9 to get out.
Maurice Hill Collection

Les Slymn

I went to Kendricks in 1964 working in the garage when Eric Smith was Foreman. He was a character. In those days we all used to wear overalls with a long ruler pocket down one side and one of his tricks was to drop a lit cigarette down this pocket when you weren't looking. All of a sudden you'd feel this heat on your leg, look down and realise you were on fire - you'd be jumping about all round the garage trying to put it out. I remember someone doing it to him once and he just walked across the garage, as calm as you like, held his pocket under the tap and turned it on.

In those days when the factory inspector was coming round we'd have to whitewash the garage. We'd do it during the day because if you were doing your job right the lorries would be out working; usually our busy time was when they started coming in at about four in the afternoon until about seven at night. Anyway, this day I'd got to do the walls and I went up the ladder with a big bucket of whitewash and a 10" brush. I'm not very good with heights so I climbed cautiously to the top. Then I sensed something and looked round and Smithy was right behind me; he'd followed me up. I was so startled that the ladder started shaking and I ended up tipping this bucket of whitewash all over him. He never bothered. I remember another trick he did was to whack anyone who walked past across the backside with the whitewash brush.

At one time Kendricks had the Dodge dealership; they had one or two Dodge flats running 'shot' out of James Bridge copper works down to Cornwall and bringing china clay up. Shortly before I went there they closed the dealership because they went over completely to Foden. I can remember working on these Dodges with Perkins engines and Boyes third axles.

Kendrick drivers were known as 'Hell Drivers' like the ones in the Stanley Baker film. There was certainly no defensive driving! I remember they used to do coal/slack down to Gloucester Power Station then down to South Wales to bring foundry coke back. Now, foundry coke is great big lumps of coke, nothing like gas coke. Anyway, the bodies had extensions on so they could get the weight on but this altered the centre of gravity of the vehicle and they'd be going along, rocking and rolling and, every so often, one would go over.

Some of the drivers would 'put the fiddle on'; they'd tamper with the governor on the engine using 'the block' or 'the specs' so that instead of 42 mph they'd be going nearer 50 mph. They'd remove these when the vehicle came into the garage because it was a sackable offence - but you could tell. This would be in the Foden Gardner 6LWs. Some of the drivers, like Jackie Booker, did the same amount of work as the others but treated the vehicles better; Jackie's truck never went wrong.

I remember Kendricks as a fantastic place to work; when I left in 1969 I went to S Jones. Horace sent for me once and asked me to go back; he told me I could have the other house that Mrs Kendrick had lived in but I didn't go. Albert Blakemore, Jackie Barrister, Teddy Gee, Sid Bishop (my brother-in-law), Graham Westley and a chap named Charlie who was the tyre-knocker were all characters who worked there the same time as me.

Jack 'Jackie' Booker, by all accounts, Kendricks' star driver. Jack had worked for Kendricks when they still had one or two horses. For a lark he used to have an alarm clock on a lavatory chain attached to the top of his overalls. *Joe Booker*

C & A FORRESTER & SONS LTD - Roger and Arnold Forrester

William Forrester moved from Ubberley Hall Farm (now shops in Bentilee) in 1881 to Red House Farm in Wolstanton. At some point he started a furniture moving business using horse-drawn, four wheel pantechnicons. They ranged as far as Derby, sleeping rough and always soaking wet. More down to earth they had the night soil and ash collection contract for Wolstanton with horses and carts. After William died his widow moved to Poplar House in Pitgreen Lane which had an attached yard and stable accessed from Lily Street. She continued the carting business from here until her sons, Charles and Alfred (Fred) returned from WW1. One contract was providing the council with horses and carts for the widening of Milehouse Lane and, of course, the loading was done by the haulier.

In the mid-1920s they acquired motor wagons; the first being the commercial version of the Ford Tin Lizzy. Charles was driving the lorries in the early days while Alfred did the maintenance and also took in outside repairs. By this time Charles's sons, Charles Jr and Arnold had joined the business. The first lorries had solid wheels and used to get stuck in the tram lines on Porthill Bank. Later, there were Ford AAs with a more conventional transmission than the two speed single pedal Tin Lizzies. There was also an early Vulcan which used to get stuck in two gears at the same time!

All the lorries had dropside tipper bodies with either balanced pivot point or hand cranked screw lift. The drop side tipper remained a feature until the end of the business in 1983. This provided for loading flints off the floor or flat work as well as regular tipper work hauling tarmac, sand, gravel or coal with the addition of top extension boards.

The fleet ran to eleven vehicles in the 1930s and Fred had to deal with with a major overhaul every weekend. This involved 'run' big ends which required him to lie on his back with the sump off, 'stropping' the big end journals before fitting new white metal bushed rods.

During the 1930s the vehicles varied from Leyland Beaver, Morris Commercial and Albion to a new 1933 ERF which was No 33 produced at Sandbach. This lorry was intended for distance flat work pulling a Dyson trailer but by the outbreak of war it was on tipper work without the tipper! After the war the chassis was shortened and a new hydraulic tipper body fitted for coal

L-R:
Arnold aged 16,
Harold and Len
with a Tin Lizzie.
Mid 1920s

work. It was started by hand cranking by Charles and Charles Jr together with a flaming torch inserted into the air intakes on cold mornings. The valves were lifted by a lever near to the cranking handle so that the flywheel could be spun before dropping the valves. Probably the valve to No1 cylinder could be dropped independently so that cylinder could be started while still hand cranking and so help start the other three cylinders. Judging by the grunts and expletives it seemed to be a Herculean task accompanied by clouds of blue smoke that filled the yard and street. The dynamo was only fitted during winter time in order to maintain the lights otherwise the battery was sufficient on its own for summer operation. The unladen weight was over 3 tons so it was limited to 20 mph.

The Albions had four cylinder petrol engines that were prone to overheating and were not very good hill climbers. In later years they used a lot of oil. When 'A' licences came along it was more economical to have fewer wagons carrying more weight and the fleet was reduced to six heavier vehicles.

During the 2nd World War the company was transporting bombs and materials for the building of aerodromes and after the war was heavily involved in coal transport. The business was too small for nationalization and operations were limited to a 50 mile radius. At this time new vehicles were scarce and ex-war Bedfords and a Commer were used on the basis of light taxation weight and maximum payload. An army rated 3 ton Bedford would be fitted with rear double tyres and helper springs. Still being under 3 ton unladen weight they would operate at 30 mph and 12 ton gross with at least an 8 ton payload.....very carefully driven! However, the Bedfords had good brakes.

At least two of the Bedfords were converted to Perkins P6 diesel by Spen Cotton Motor Engineers. However, the gearboxes used to suffer; second gear regularly losing teeth. The wagon was kept working, missing out second gear. A spare box was kept overhauled and used to be interchanged when the wagon came in at the end of a working day with no running time lost.

Two Canadian ex WD Dodges were also acquired and uprated like the ex WD Bedfords to operate at 12 tons gross and 30 mph. They had two speed Eaton axles and transmission parking brakes which were sometimes used to augment the poor wheel brakes. Unfortunately, in one case leading to a prop shaft breaking when pulling up to a halt on a steep hill whilst loaded. The engine stalled so the driver had no servo assistance and he had to steer backwards with next to no brakes down the hill, through traffic. Fortunately, there was no damage to vehicles or pedestrians.

At some stage they acquired an ex WD ERF light six wheeler chassis with a 4LW Gardner and double drive rear axles fitted with a tipper body; it performed well with a good payload but the rear springs were awkward to refit.

In the 1951 a new 8 ton Vulcan was purchased from Beech's. This had power hydraulic brakes driven by belts off the back of the gear box which was fine at speed but hopeless when going slow. The 1933 ERF was scrapped in 1952 after 19 years' service and the brake compressor and Clayton servo were later fitted to the Vulcan by Spen Cotton Motor Engineers who had taken over the bigger repairs.

Charles and Alfred retired in 1954 and Arnold passed away the same year. This left Charles Jr to run the business. From the mid-1950s there were 4 four wheelers and 2 six wheelers until the company was wound up in 1983. Throughout the 50s and 60s a large proportion of the work was transporting sand and gravel from Trentham Gravel, Willowbridge, to Liverpool, Manchester and various power stations. Three trips a day to Liverpool was not unusual in vehicles that struggled to do 20 mph. However, it was good running across the Cheshire plain except for Budworth Bank and Hatton Hill on the way to Meaford - this is where I learnt to get in crawler in the ERF. I (Roger)

Arnold in his 20s. This could be an Albion. c1930   L-R: Arnold, Caroline and Charles Jr.

The ERF purchased in 1933 which was run for 19 years
until 1952. It was used for general purpose haulage.
George Pritchard Collection

Roger c1962 in his Dodge
six-wheeler with Leyland
Comet engine. Taken at the
Wolstanton yard.

shouldn't have been driving but I used to persuade Jeff Cope!

The vehicles were mainly Dodge and Big Bedfords with an ERF six wheeler which was sold by Beech's as a light six with trailing axle and 5 cylinder Gardner. It actually weighed over 8 tons and could carry only just 12 ton under the 20 ton gross regulations. It was used for 10 years and ended up off road on the M6 construction after being fitted with double drive axles by the man who bought it.

The Vulcan was the company's first post-war lorry purchased from Beech's. This version was only manufactured for two years under Rootes Group.

The replacement Dodge six wheelers were much better at 6 ton unladen weight, carrying 14 tons. The first new Dodge six-legger was a 'Kew' (parrot nose) model with Perkins R6 and Boyes trailing axle. It was very fast but the engine was short lived. Later Dodge models had Leyland Comet 350 and 375 engines with 5 speed DB boxes, Eaton two speed axles, power steering and cab heaters - considered flyers and looked good!

Most of the drivers were local to the garage, in fact Harold Forrester (cousin of Charles and Arnold) lived at Poplar House at the bottom of the yard and drove for the whole of his life for the business except for driving an ambulance in WW2 at the front in Germany. He had a SWB Bedford O type which nobody else drove. This lorry was eventually sold to Ken Sturge so his 17 year old son Alan could drive it. I remember being a little bit jealous at the time; I think I was 16.

Some of the other drivers were Harry McBeth (he later drove for Jim Frost over the wall in James Street) and Vic Wild. Harry Crank from James Street drove an Albion during the war and later the Vulcan after Arnold's death in 1954. Sid Machin, Arthur Walker, Jeff Cope and Lofty Stevenson drove for many years. Two drivers were exceptionally allowed to take their lorries home as they lived near Trentham Gravel, Charlie Machin from Ashley and Sid Edwards from Pipe Gate.

Alan Sturge remembers his father taking him to collect this. Harold took him to one side and told him to look after it. Alan opened the door and looked inside and it was like new even though it was 11 years old.
Alan Sturge Collection

All photos, unless otherwise stated, *Forrester Collection.*

GEORGE DEAKIN

Driving had always been in my life and in my blood. This came from my dad, Thomas Deakin, who drove all his life for J Rogerson. My story starts in 1961 when I was 17 and got my first driving job with Whitmore Brothers Builders Merchants based at Station Yard, Cobridge. They had two lorries back then: a Bedford 'O' type and a Commer Q4 Tipper. I was delivering building materials in the local area.

After roughly 12 months I moved to a job at Hodgkiss Dairy of Lovatt Street, Stoke where I was employed as a driver and semi-skilled mechanic. This had me still in the local area but also included working in the yard, looking after their fleet of four Thorneycroft flatbeds. I used to go out at 3.30am every morning to Calveley to collect a load of sterilised milk for the depot; this was unloaded into the fridges for distribution. Once this daily task was completed I'd go on to servicing and repairing the lorries to keep them roadworthy.

I worked at Hodgkiss for just over 12 months before joining Joseph Kimberley of Sutherland Road, Longton, driving Leyland Comets and six wheeled Bedford TKs. I mainly worked on materials from the open cast coal mine in Cheadle whether it be coal or rock salt, which I went on to deliver all over the UK. I also did some night driving for them with an artic tanker, a Leyland Beaver, delivering silica sand to the whole of the North East.

At 21 I moved to BRS. I was a young lad compared to the rest of the drivers but because my Dad's mates at BRS put in a good word for me, they gave me a job. This was a big step up for me as I'd only been used to driving a couple of different vehicles with my previous jobs whereas here I was spoilt for choice: Bristol, Leyland Octopus, Seddon, Leyland Comet and AEC Mercury and Mandator. I was moving steel out of Shelton Bar from Etruria; Rist Wires and Cables at Milehouse, Newcastle; insulators out of Bullers at Milton; copper out of Thomas Bolton at Froghall; tyres out of Michelin in Stoke and sanitary ware out of Twyfords of Etruria. I also used to move combine harvesters from Tring in Hertfordshire all the way to the north of Scotland.

George in his BRS days with a Leyland.

Two years later I moved to Wild Condon. Working for Vic Wild had me tramping again; carrying anything and everything all over the country in an ERF KV. I had a turbulent time working for him and told him to 'lick 'em and stick 'em' twice and moved on to work for Beresfords and Tideswells but after these breaks I moved back and was one of five drivers that Vic supported in becoming self-employed. I hired my unit and trailer to work for myself whilst still having the security of working for him. Vic then spoke to Frank Caulkin to hire me a Mickey Mouse Foden from Valences of Newton Abbot in Devon. One Saturday Dave Unwin visited my house in Baddeley Green and said that he used to drive this lorry at Valences and that one day he would buy it; he was starting with Unique Car Sales. I should have guessed that something would happen. Frank Caulkin rang me on the following Monday night to tell me that there was no longer a unit to hire as Dave Unwin had bought it. This left me with plenty of work but no vehicle to drive so I had to go out and buy my own unit and trailer. I did a deal with Jack Critchlow of Mow Cop for a Scammell Handyman which also included some work from Charcon Derby and some through Sammy Williams moving steel coils from Dagenham Docks. Leaving Vic, becoming self-employed and setting up my own business begins a whole new story!

I started totally on my own in late 1971 when I got some work for Staffs Public Works, Stoke, sub-contracting for J Rogerson. Then I went on contract for Chapman & Ball shunting trailers all over England which were loading for the Middle East. One day Jack Corrie said I would have to go to Vienna with an urgent load of plastic footballs. So off I went with my non-sleeper Scammell Handyman on to the ferry for my first venture into driving abroad! I did another couple of trips overseas - St Poulton and Belgium - and then carried on shunting in the UK. One day Jack said I had to go to Tehran. I said that there was no chance in my Scammell so I paid a visit to my mate Dave Unwin at Unique Car Sales and told him I was looking for a Scania - urgently!! Dave phoned a friend in Bolton who had four that were ex Sammy Williams. We went up to see him at 8.30 the next day where I picked a six wheel unit and Dave did a deal with him. We picked it up, taxed and insured it and I spent the Saturday servicing it before leaving on the Sunday afternoon with Derek Owen, another of Chapman and Ball's owner drivers, for Dover and my first trip to Tehran.

This was the Scania, ex Sammy Williams, that George bought off Dave Unwin.

After that first trip I ended up doing $2^1/2$ years on the Middle East runs. In about 1976 I started what turned out to be a 26 year contract with Simpsons Potters which saw them incorporating me into the bricks and mortar of their factory-even going to the lengths of building me my own fitting shop within the old mould making building. A large contract that Simpsons landed with Tefal saw me loading up a trailer every Saturday and setting out on the Sunday for Southern France.

My wife, Janet, has always been very supportive. She would help with repairs and maintenance as well as doing all the bookwork. If it hadn't been for Janet I wouldn't have achieved as much as I did.

By 1989 our business had expanded and my daughter, Elizabeth, was driving our Mercedes 307 van for daily deliveries to Brailsford Pottery in Derby and pretty soon going further afield for them. When she was 21 she passed her Class 1 HGV and was driving a Leyland Freighter and later a Ford Cargo. Other contracts for JCB and Remploy kept us busy and at weekends we were both busy completing servicing and repairs on the vehicles.

The chairman of Simpsons lived in Arizona where he also ran Simpsons' sister company, Catalina China. When he came to the UK I was assigned as his chauffeur to drive him to and from Heathrow and his business meetings. I was also a key holder to the flat he kept in Newcastle under Lyme. Eventually, he decided to wind down the business in the UK and concentrate his retiring years on his smaller company in the USA. This, unfortunately, left us continually trying to battle with larger haulage companies for work to keep both Liz and myself busy.

At this point Liz decided to retrain to find a new career and left the company to go to

George with BRS Seddon.

A BRS AEC

A BRS Bristol

George (R) in front of his Scania. We don't know the name of the other man.

university; this enabled me to keep working at a steady rate, but then, due to high fuel and maintenance costs and the growing number of haulage companies vying for work I came to the decision to sell my vehicles and contract my time out. It kept me in the profession I had enjoyed for the majority of my working life. I then drove abnormal loads and sometimes their escort vehicles and 'kit' houses around the UK - so I kept 'truckin' until my retirement!

Liz Deakin

Dad was abroad for a lot of my young life but I always went down to the yard with him when he was home. I can remember driving tractor units around the yard from a young age and I used to go under them helping with repairs. Sometimes when he was out and about on deliveries in this country Mum and I would go with him and we'd all camp out in the back of the lorry in the middle of the load. I have been abroad with him but I was too young to remember. He used to send me postcards from the Middle East 'To my little Rubber Duck' which was a reference to 'Convoy' the seventies hit record about a group of truckers crossing America who communicated by CB.

A John Heath photo. John spotted George on Michael Wood services on M5. Early 1990s. The 'L' plate was for Liz.

ABOVE
Taken in the yard at Simpsons Potters. On the left is Liz's Leyland with Ford Cargo on the right.

LEFT
George's wife, Janet(left) with Liz in front of George's ERF at Truckfest, Peterborough

When I left school I went to Sumlock Business School and after that to a company on a Youth Training Scheme. After a while the company was bought out and I went on short time. At this time Dad's business was really taking off so I would help him on my days off and eventually went to work for him full-time.

When I first worked for Dad I was driving a van and then went on to a seven and a half tonner. It was around this time that I started going to truck shows; I won a couple of awards for my truck and got to know a lot of people in the business. In 1991 I passed my Class 1 and drove a Leyland. Quite often when I was driving along people would pass and do a double-take when they saw a woman driving a lorry. Sometimes they'd start a conversation on the CB and when I said I was working for my dad they'd say something like, 'Oh, so you've had to do it, then.' I'd say, 'No, I want to do it.' Occasionally drivers

Liz again with her Leyland in Simpson's yard.
All photos *Deakin Collection* unless stated otherwise.

would say I was getting special treatment, particularly when I got to the destination and was waiting to tip. If they got me in a bit earlier some of them would say it was because I was a woman. It wasn't. Dad had always told me 'the customer is king' so I was polite and never moaned about changes or delays. If I had to wait I'd find something to do like hoovering the cab!

I was once out on the road when I developed a problem with my gear box and stopped on a lay-by. I was under the wagon checking that it still had fluid in when I heard a vehicle pull up behind then someone walking towards me. I came out and this guy says 'Oh, have you got problems, Drive?' He was as nice as pie then all of a sudden he just turned and went to grab me. I tried to get in the cab but I couldn't get the door to shut because he was in the way. Eventually, I think something distracted him and he turned so I shoved him and managed to close the door. Up until that time I'd always thought of myself as one of the lads and had never been afraid. I was really shocked. Obviously, I noted the name of the company and the registration number. When I got home I didn't say anything at first but my mum knew something was wrong. When I told her she phoned the company and reported him. After that I would always take Benji our Doberman/Alsation with me in the cab.

After working for Dad for about 15 years the company we were on contract for began working short weeks. This was a hard time for the business and to save Dad struggling to find work for both of us I decided to leave and pursue a different path

I'd always been interested in Forensic Science so I enrolled at University and graduated in 2007 with a BSc (hons) Forensic Science and in 2009 an MSc. I now work full time at the University. I haven't forgotten my driving roots as I took on the challenge of taking my Minibus Driving Permit and regularly take groups of students out and about on field trips.

Liz Degree no. 3!
2012

IAN TAYLOR

My earliest memory of riding in a lorry was in the 1950s when, as a schoolboy walking home from school in Newcastle to Silverdale, I was given a lift by a neighbour in a red Bedford tipper truck taking coal from Newcastle to Crewe. The firm was Rutland Transport.

I left school in 1958 and joined the army in 1962. When I finished in 1969 I was a tank driving instructor. My first driving job was for John Copestake at Cooke and Copestake in Smallwood. The firm was owned by John and Eric Cooke; Eric's brother, Percy, was the firm's mechanic. They ran about six trucks: three 4 wheelers, a 6 wheeled Albion driven by an Irishman named Des Carroll, and two Albion artics. One of these artics was driven by 'Acker' Bilk. Eric Cooke also had a connection with another firm, Cooke and Cotton, with just one vehicle, a 6 wheeled Albion tipper on coal work, driven by Tommy Gater.

I started off in a Bedford TK 4 wheeler which was hardly good enough for the long-distances we were doing and the weights we were carrying. Most of the work was for Triplex glass out of St Helens to the Ford Works at Dagenham. A lot of return loads were cowhides from slaughter houses around the country to a leather tannery at Nantwich. Then we used to load the finished product out to different leather users around the country. I did this job for quite a few months until the vehicle failed. At that time the firm had one artic, an Albion Chieftain, but they'd got another on order. The new one had been delayed so I had an AEC Mandator artic on loan from Tillotsons for a while. That was my first year in a class 1, as it is now. Anyway, the older driver had the new one when it arrived and I had his old motor, an Albion Chieftain artic, single axle trailer running at 24 tons.

A period as a mechanic at Chatfields followed where I was offered the job of Foreman in the truck shop. The others moaned about me being promoted because I was so young but they'd all turned the job down! After about 18 months I went to work for Vic Wild. My uncle, Harry McBeth, was working there at the time and got me the job. Uncle Harry, incidentally, had been in transport since the 1920's and had been 'second man' on the Model T Ford that Arnold Forester had driven when they were both 16! He'd also driven Foden steamers and chain-drive Scammells before working for Vic.

I soon proved my ability at Wilds and got on quite well. I was one of the people who joined Vic's 'owner driver' scheme. Vic was a dyed in the wool Gardner man and all the trucks at the time, ERF's and Atkinsons, had the Gardner 180. When the new Gardner 240 engine came out, there was a changeover for the owner drivers to one of the new trucks. I was due for the next one when Gardners went on strike and the supply of new trucks with Gardner 240's dried up. Then Vic saw an ERF in Herman Tideswell's colours with a 240 Gardner. He knew that Herman had always been an AEC man so he rang Gardners and told them where to stick their engines and promptly bought 3 new DAF 2600's, of which I had the first one on the road.

I was actually quite successful as an owner-driver and got a direct contract working for English China Clays. Even Vic, who did the same work, couldn't get it direct so I was on a better rate than him. Anyway, he told me that all payments had to go through his office so he could have a cut - and his cut was quite a lot! - or I'd have to park the vehicle up. So, I parked the truck in the middle of the yard and said 'I'll see you then, Vic'. He said, 'Aren't you going to wash it off?' I told him, 'It's not mine, it's yours - you wash it off!'

I went back to the garage trade for a month or two before getting a job as a driver for Carmans. For the first month I was pulling unaccompanied trailers out of Dover delivering around the country, loading and taking them back to Dover. However, I got back to the yard one Friday and the boss

This picture was taken in about 1973/74 when Ian was tramping for Vic.
This was Ian's first European truck, before this he had driven an Atki.

asked me if I'd got a passport. When I told him I had he said he'd got a trip for me the following week to.... Baghdad! I thought he was joking. I didn't know at the time that they did Middle East.

When the Middle East work started it was because these Arab countries were facing huge delays in getting their orders because there was only one deep sea port on the Arabian Peninsular at that time. As a consequence, any ships going out were anchoring up off-shore for as long as twelve months, paying the crews off and waiting for a berth to get the ship in. So, all of a sudden, someone thought about road transport. We were competing with sea transport but it was no more expensive so people were literally buying fleets of trucks to do this work. The Middle East work really took off in the mid 70s.

Carmans' biggest customer at the time was Twyfords at Alsager, and we were taking toilets and bathroom suites out to Iraq, Iran and Syria - all over the place, really. This would be about 1975. Anyway, the truck I was using for the journey to Baghdad was the one I'd used for shunting; a Volvo F88 240 ex-European lorry that had been retired to work in the UK. I spent a week in the garage with the fitters preparing it for the journey. I went with two other guys who'd done European work and I had driven abroad before when I spent three years in Germany with the forces. So the three of us, Bob Matthews, John Mudd, (both with brand new Volvo F88 290's,) and I, set out 'hand-in-hand' because none of us had been to the Middle East before.

It was a steep learning curve because when we got to Baghdad we found out we'd missed a Customs check. We should have called at Mosel in Iraq but nobody had told us. Anyway, they sent us the 250 miles back to Mosel where we were hauled up in front of the Chief of Customs and asked why we shouldn't be put into jail for smuggling. We pleaded ignorance so they let us off and sent us on our way. In those days the Baghdad Customs was just a few tents in the desert at Abu Ghraib where the big prison is, on the outskirts of Baghdad before a dedicated Customs facility was built at Al Fallujah, about thirty miles outside Baghdad. I remember it was April/May when we went out and it was so hot. Anyway, we were loaded back from Germany and when we arrived back in the UK we'd been away for five weeks.

I said I wanted to go to Baghdad again now I knew how to do it, so Bob and I went out. I had inherited John Mudd's Volvo F88 290 this time and it was the best time I've ever done a Middle East in; just over three weeks there and back for an 8000 mile round trip. Not bad.

After that I delivered to Baghdad several times. Whenever I got back to the yard there would be several trailers loaded for various destinations and I would be asked, 'Where do you want to go now?' Eventually, I said I'd like to go to Kuwait. I'd got to the stage where I was confident to go on my own. Even if you were running with someone you couldn't be sure you'd see them again so once you got to the border you'd tell them where you planned to stay. It had to be a loose arrangement as traffic conditions dictated that you couldn't be sure of staying together. Also it wasn't a good idea to stick around if one of you was involved in an accident as, being a foreigner, you'd get pulled in to it as well.

Ian took this of his companions, John Mudd (sitting) and Bob Matthews on their first trip to Baghdad.

I remember an occasion when I was en route to Tehran, crossing Eastern Turkey. leading another driver on his first trip. We were climbing the Tahir pass which is twice the height of Snowdon and is only a dirt road when this Turkish bus overtook me and pulled across to block my progress. The other driver had dropped behind about a half a mile. Anyway, all the passengers disembarked and surrounded my truck indicating that I had held them up - they weren't happy! Unfortunately, the Ford Transcon I was driving had no means of locking the cab door from the inside and the bus driver opened my door and tried to drag me from the cab. The passengers were drawing their fingers across their throats as a threat.

I always carried a large knife in the cab in case I needed it but I knew that if I drew it I would have to be prepared to use it. Anyway, my instinct for survival when faced with 30 angry Turks in a place like Eastern Turkey, was to arm myself. However, just in the nick of time the other driver pulled up behind me. All of a sudden the Turks decided to get back on the bus with the driver still waving his fist at me as he left. I often think what would have happened if the other driver hadn't arrived when he did.

After Carman's I went to Chapman and Ball until it closed down and then drove for Litcor International for about a year, again to the Middle East. Initially, though, it was tipping work for B J Waters of Matlock, including some European work tipping in Holland or Germany and loading back crushed iron ore from Germany to Bedford.

After Litcor I drove for Expo Freight in Loughton in Essex doing Middle East work and then Transleam International in Margate running mainly to Turkey.

By 1986 the Middle East work was declining and you couldn't earn as much. My brother, who had an engineering firm, offered me a three month trial so I left driving and went into engineering. I stayed for 18 years before retiring at 60. However, after a few weeks I became restless and signed on at an agency for driving work and have been doing two nights a week for Fedex ever since.

I took a lot of photographs during my 12 years as a driver in the Middle East and enjoy giving talks to local groups about my adventures. I'm also writing a book *My Middle East*.

Ian's F88 parked outside the Harem Hotel, Istanbul.

ABOVE
Ian taken just
outside Baghdad
on his first trip.

RIGHT
Ian with Expo
Freight Scania
at a truck stop
en route to
Tehran.

RIGHT
Bob Matthews
unloading at a
battery factory,
Baghdad 1975.

ABOVE
Taken in 1979 at Thessalonika Docks,
Greece. Mercedes SK.

LEFT
My semi-retirement vehicle

BELOW
1979. Mercedes SK on tipping work at
Port Talbot Steelworks.
All photos *Ian Taylor*

IAN ADAMS

I started driving for Ernie Owen when I was 21; he signed the form for me to get my licence. When I got the job I didn't know anything so I rang Ray Gould and told him I'd got to go to Scotland the next night and hadn't got a clue! Ray was at Mountford Brothers so we went across to their yard and he dropped a trailer and put it back again and showed me how to couple-up etc.

Ian (left) with Ray Gould doing the washing up in Mo Camp, Iran.

After I while I went back to butchering - I had a shop in Cobridge but then I put a manager in and went on Beresfords because I wanted to do Continental. They gave me an ERF with a 150 Gardner; no sleeper, magic board. I went on my own because I didn't want anyone with me. The first time I went to the Middle East I went on my own too; it took me a lot longer but I preferred it.

I remember once when I was on Thor I went with this driver and he dumped his wagon. He was a great big youth and he was saying what he was going to do and acting big but he was like a big girl, really. We got down to Istanbul and Alan, the manager, had done a block booking for a couple or three days at the Harem Hotel. Anyway, this youth says 'I'm going home tomorrow' and didn't care about the wagon. I ended up giving him a thump. We'd both got a load of saucepans on for Baghdad and should have gone together but he caught the plane and went home.

When he got back he went to the yard to see Alan and he'd got this great big bloke with him. So Alan says 'What do you want?' and he says 'I've come for my money?' and he turns to this big bloke and says 'And what do you want?' 'I've come to see he gets it.' Alan says 'You get outside them XXXX gates right now; I don't want you on the XXXX premises.' He turned round and went out - Alan breathed a sigh of relief! This driver had cost the firm a lot of money because Alan had to get Jack Morley to fly out to Istanbul, get the wagon and deliver the load to Baghdad.

Ian parked up Iroun, 1970s. *Photos Ian Adams*

SHIRLEY'S TRANSPORT - Arthur Shirley

My dad, Jim Shirley, started the business in 1936 after he'd quit his job as a coal bagger for a firm in Ash Bank. He left when he discovered his co-worker was being paid half a crown more than him; this was hard to take especially as he had to go to this man's house every morning to get him up! When he challenged the boss he was told 'If you don't like it, you know what you can do.'

So Dad decided to set up on his own but as he didn't have any money he asked his father to lend him £200 to buy a vehicle. The answer was 'Yes, but my name goes on it - G W Shirley & Sons.' He insisted that Dad's brother, who was in the army at the time, came into the business too.

The first vehicle was a Bedford and it was kept at Waste Farm, Rownall, which was where grandfather lived. Dad had to work hard to get the business off the ground; he managed to secure a contract for the War Ministry and was delivering bread during the night. By this time he'd met my mother, Lily Clarke, who lived in Shelton. Mum was working at Twyfords at the time but was also helping with the business. They married in about 1942 and lived at Waste Farm until they moved to Mount Pleasant Farm, Cellarhead.

The business grew and they started hauling cattle and delivering meat to butchers, taking bagged corn to farmers and doing lime spreading. Obviously this meant working very long hours and when my uncle came out of the army and joined the firm, he wasn't prepared to do it. This didn't go down well with my mother and she eventually gave Dad an ultimatum to finish the partnership or else! So Dad didn't have a lot of choice but to go on his own. It was a struggle because he had to give up some of the vehicles - they probably had about five or six at the time - and money was tight. Dad bought Mount Pleasant Farm, where the business is based now, in 1944, and in about 1948 he split with his brother. My uncle carried on in transport so there was a bit of rivalry between them because they both had meat wagons, but eventually my uncle went in to coal bagging.

My eldest brother, James was born at Waste Farm and I was born at Mount Pleasant as was my younger brother, Reg. My father continued to expand the business which was by now Shirley's Transport. He used to do a lot of work for Baxter's Butchers who had a shop more or less in every town within a 50 mile radius of Stoke. He'd go out with a full load of meat from Weddell's, Towers or Stoke Cold Store delivering to Shrewsbury and Church Stretton and coming back through Newport; it was a full day. The Macclesfield round could have as many as 50 shops in a day and it was all loaded and unloaded by the drivers and drivers' mates - no hydraulic hoists in those days. They'd carry the meat into the shops and, as in the case of Stoke Market, they'd park as near as they could and walk down the street with half a pig or whatever on their shoulders. Eventually this work dropped off as farmers started having their own cattle trucks and trailers and butchers had their own vans.

In the late 1950s we went into general haulage

Thorneycroft cattle wagon purchased new. c1949. *Shirley Collection*

and in the early 1960s we dropped lucky by working for Allied Breweries in Burton going to their depots in Plymouth, Torquay and Truro and north to Warrington, Leeds and Manchester. We were carrying beer in kegs and crates and returning with empties. When we went on the beer job it was good for the men because they'd get to their destination and would only have to take the sheet off as they were unloaded by forklift - all the driver had to do was put the empties on and sheet up. It was pretty well-known that if you went to work for Shirley's it was hard work because it was mainly carry-on/carry-off but with the brewery work they had it easier - they could be dressed-up all the time! When the drivers knew they'd got a Torquay they'd be on the phone booking a bed at the digs; there was no roughing it. This work began to decline in the 1970s when the M5 was built because Allied opened a new depot at Avonmouth and started to trunk their own beer down.

In 1963 we became involved with some customers who bought and sold tallow in 45 gallon drums. That's when our business really opened up and we started going to London and Liverpool carrying these drums. We had Bedfords at first with the odd Sentinel, Thorneycroft and Dodge but in 1963 we started with Albions.

I used to go to the yard from a very young age; I was driving by the time I was eight and drove nearly everything we had. I remember there was only one vehicle Dad didn't like me driving and that was a twin-steer ERF. When I left school I wanted to be a driver's mate but my mother wouldn't hear of it; I had to work in the office. As soon as I was 17 I had a lucky break, literally, when one of the drivers broke his wrist. The 'L' plates went on and this driver, Freddie Fenton from Bucknall, sat passenger while I drove. Anyway, two weeks after my17th birthday I passed my test. Freddie, who was a tiny man in his sixties, wasn't happy because now I didn't need anyone to sit with me. The men knew Dad as well as I did so he wasn't surprised when Dad said 'Freddie, you'd better go on the club!' I think my first solo trip was probably to Manchester for a load of corn.

Dad did a lot of work for Woolliscroft Butchers; he'd taken over their wagons when they decided they didn't want to do it themselves. At the time we were already doing their distance work taking tallow in drums to firms like Colgate and Palmolive as well as Levers at Port Sunlight, Drury's at Brighouse and Cousins at Nottingham. The manager of Woolliscroft's, Albert Adams from Ash Bank, had known my mum and dad for many years I remember he was the only person outside the family who was allowed to call my mother Lily. He phoned her one day and said, 'Lily, I've had a word with your Jim and he isn't listening; tankers are the future not these drums. What we're going to be doing here is having a bulk tank store with tankers coming in to take the stuff away. You should be ready because this is the future.' This was in 1966. Anyway, she persuaded Dad and he bought a second hand Andrews rigid tank off an eight wheeler and I went with him to Antcliffe's in Manchester to fetch it. I asked, 'What are you going to put under it?' I thought we were in for a big wagon; at the time we hadn't got any eight wheelers, the biggest we'd had were Albion and ERF six wheelers. He said, 'You'll be driving it, lad. We're going to get you a new Albion six wheeler.' At that time we could go to 22 ton gross on these Albions. I said. 'But this is off an eight wheeler, 24 ton gross; we're going to be overloaded.' 'Only a bit!' he said.

When I had the Albion tank I had nobody to ask how it worked; I had to learn as I went along. I remember Dad bought a second-hand cargo pump. We'd put the tank on the chassis and he says 'I've got a pump.' He gave it to me and it wouldn't turn. I said, 'What use is this?' He said, 'By the time you've stripped it down and got it working you'll know all about it so when you have a breakdown you'll be able to repair it... .because it's no good ringing me.'

I remember going to Hertfordshire in this Albion for a load of hog fat. It was a hot day and

1966 Albion
pictured outside
Arthur's home at
Kingsley.

Shirley Collection

I'd got out of Hitchin and was driving along when I noticed this motorist trying to catch my attention. Eventually, I pulled up and got out. I walked to the back of the vehicle and was sprayed by this fat; it was spurting out like a fountain. It must have got so hot inside the tank that the pressure had built up and pushed the gasket out. I climbed on top and opened the lid to release the pressure and it went down fairly quickly. So now, instead of this fat spraying out, it was pouring on to the road. Well, I didn't know what to do. I found a pair of old overalls in the cab and wrapped them round the gasket as best I could and secured them with string. I drove about half mile down the road, parked up and went back into Hitchin to find a phone box to ring home.

Dad came to the phone 'What's up?' I told him what had happened and I'll never forget what he said. 'Well, it's a simple as this, lad, you're there and I'm here. Go back and see what you can do but, as I say, you're there and I'm here.' That was it. I was on my own.

I went back and the fat had started to congeal slightly. I remember there was a 'T' adapter that should have had a pressure relief valve and the old chap had had me plugging this hole with a piece of wood. I thought about it and came to the conclusion that this was the problem so I took it out. I'd got to get to Birkenhead and decided to take the risk; it wasn't a full load and I drove very steadily and eventually arrived at my destination. I came straight back because we'd got to sort the problem and put a gasket in. I said to Dad when I got back 'It needs a valve it's that piece of wood that's the problem!' Anyway, we bought a new valve and fitted it and it was OK after that.

I started to get to know a bit about the job and kept pestering the old chap to get an ERF artic like Smith and Robinson's were running and he eventually agreed. He ordered one and it came in August 1968 but was parked up for ages until we'd got something for it to pull. I had to look at this ERF standing in the yard for about three months! Anyway, he ordered a new Butterfield tank and I remember going to fetch it with my parents on November 7th. We should have gone to get it early in the morning but there was a delay. The weather was bad; not snowing but icy underfoot. At about 4.00 in the afternoon I climbed in the cab to drive back with this tanker on and Dad said to me, 'Remember, thay'st got a lot of work to do before the day's finished. Thay'st got a vehicle that's worth more than my bloody house.... and it bends in the middle. Once we're out of this area I'll put my foot down and be gone; dunner hang about - but be careful.'

When I got back I had to put flexes and fittings on the tank, refuel and check wheel nuts and tyre pressures. Then I'd got to go and load. It was about midnight and I thought I'd just pop home, get cleaned up and have something to eat. I knew I could tip at British Celanese, because they were open all night and then down to Wellingborough early in the morning and I'd be back on target. Then Dad starts again with 'Hast done the tyre pressures? And the wheel nuts?'

Before I left Dad said 'Now, everything's brand new, as you well know, and there's a filter in that pump. I dunner want you loadin' without that filter in. I dunner want anythin' coming up and knockin' that pump about.' Well, that morning at Wellingborough, I was loading this fat and there was plenty of air. I was pumping for a short while and it was clogged up. All new to me, of course. The pipes were jumping about and, as it was chain-driven on the gear box, the chain was rattling and snatching. So I stopped it, got a torch and could see it was clogged. I got my tools out and took it to bits. It wasn't a filter I could just take out, I had to take the flanges off and then wash it out and put it back on. It did it again and again and I'm thinking about the old man and this bloody filter. In the end I just took the filter out and filled up. I don't think I ever had it in again. Dad used to come round the yard and look at things and one day he said 'What have I told you about having no filter - how long's it been like this?' I said, 'From day one!'

It was all a steep learning curve but the business really took off in 1972. That's when my life changed. One day, when we were having dinner, I said, 'I want another tanker.' My mother said 'There are no more tankers coming here; I can't cope any longer in the office.' She would probably have been in her late fifties then. It wasn't an easy job in the office; sometimes loads would be rejected and they'd say 'You're not tipping in Manchester, you're tipping in Leeds.' I once had a load on for a full week. Anyway, we reached a compromise - we would have another tanker but I'd have to come off the road and work in the office. I didn't want to but I had no choice. I used to keep my hand in with the driving by doing holiday relief work.

Shirley family
L-R: Veronica, James, Reg, Jim (Chairman of Cheadle Council), Lily, Arthur and Ann. This picture was taken in the 1960s. Sadly, in 1970 Reg was fatally injured when the tanker he was driving was involved in an accident on the M6.
Shirley Collection.

ERF B Series, fleet
no. 99 'The Wizard'.
Seen coupled to the
yard shunter.
Carl Johnson

ABOVE
ERF C Series, fleet no. 111
in John Wyatt livery.
Carl Johnson

LEFT
DAF 95XF480 fleet no. 180.
Carl Johnson

Classic Volvo F88, fleet no. 84 'Grace' originally a 4 x 2 unit but was converted to a 6 x 2 fitted with tag axle. Terry Lewis drove this.
Carl Johnson

ABOVE
Foden Alpha 420 coupled to tipping trailer used on local quarry work.
Carl Johnson

RIGHT
A rare motor for Shirley's IVECO Eurotech.
Carl Johnson

My father died in August 1985 and my mother in January 1986. My brother, James who lives next door to the garage has always been involved in the business; he served an apprenticeship at Tom Byatt's at Fenton then came here when he was 21. He's always worked in the garage, but he has retired now through ill-health.

About twelve months before my mother died I remember her saying to us 'When we're not here I don't want you buying vehicle after vehicle. There's towards 30 vehicles here; you should be able to live off these comfortably'. I didn't listen because we've been up to as many as 87 vehicles. We've got about 70 now.

Ray Gould

I went to work for Shirley's in about 1996. It was all tanker work and as I hadn't done it before someone had to come with me the first time to show me the ropes. Anyway, Arthur (Shirley) came on that first trip to Manchester. We arrived and I'd got to load. Arthur says, 'Right, Ray, you've got to get on top of the wagon.' So I climb up and there was a big pipe, like an arm, that used to come swinging round. Well, it was full of oil but I didn't know. Anyway, when it came round you were supposed to hold it up so it doesn't all come out. Nobody told me. Round it comes and I go straight underneath and it goes over the top and whoosh, all over the floor. Arthur says, 'I've never seen that before. Normally, when that arm comes round it covers the driver with oil.' I looked at him and said 'And you'd have let that happen to me? Well, you'd be on the floor with it!' He laughed his head off. He said 'You'll get used to it, Ray.' Anyway, we got down to Fuchs and unloaded and he says 'Right, I'm off. Do you know what you're doing?' I said 'You've got to come with me, haven't you? We've got to go to Stanlow now.' 'Oh, you'll be OK.' I said 'Don't you want me to wait here until they come to pick you up?' He said 'I bloody don't want you to wait here - get off and earn me some money, will you!'

Ray Gould delivering oil to a ship at Liverpool Docks.
Photo Ray Gould

**Volvo taken at Croxden
Gravel c 1994.**
Shirley Collection

**Arthur showing support for the RHA's
campaign on fuel prices for British Hauliers.**
Shirley Collection

**In 1989 Arthur bought out Jeff Harrison.
This was one of the lorries driven by Steve
Sheldon. Shirley Collection**

Arthur's grandson, Jordan, in the Volvo F10 he has restored. Jordan works for his father. *Shirley Collection*

Scania 580 V8 driven until recently by Gary Shirley. *John Heath*

1940s. Sentinel cattle truck, reg ORF 59. Shirley's had this from new. It was the only Sentinel the company ever had because it proved to be unsuitable the animal effluent seeped through onto the engine which was under the chassis! Arthur can remember when they'd have two cattle wagons coming down from Buxton into Leek - the Sentinel would be in front attached by a tow chain to the one behind to hold it back. The driver in the picture is Joe Spooner, seen here in the white coat. *Carl Johnson Collection.*

1950s. Taken on the forecourt at Shirley's.
L-R: Stan Poole, Bedford 5 ton OWD; George Wilshaw, Bedford 5 ton OLBD; Freddie Fenton, Bedford S Model 7 tonner with Perkins P6 engine.
Shirley Collection

2012. Bill Crombie (L) and Clayton King standing with two vehicles from the present fleet, Shirley's yard. *John Heath*

G ALCOCK HAULIERS OF BURSLEM Reg Alcock

My dad started the business with his dad in 1931 using a 35 cwt vehicle they'd bought from the Coal Board for £11. This came about because Dad was working for Maddocks pot bank with a horse and cart and was injured. He was coming out of Anderton Wharf one day when the horse dropped dead and the shafts fell across him. He was quite badly injured and was off work for quite a while. When he was better and wanted to go back they wouldn't have him so he and granddad started the business.

They had a yard in Lyndhurst Street and their first job was carrying stone from Bakewell. They also had one or two horses that they used for carting shraff for the pot banks. When I was old enough I went into the business as did my brothers, Roy and Ernest. We had a coal round as well and I can remember Roy and Ern delivering coal in wheelbarrows. We also had a taxi business; we had a big Hillman, a Humber and an Armstrong Sidley Sapphire. When granddad died he left the business to dad and his three brothers, George, Arthur and Harry and their sister, Lizzie Peppiatt.

On the haulage side we did a lot of work for Goldendale which was owned by W.E. Dunne who had started out with a wheelbarrow in Wednesbury. He became a very wealthy man but you wouldn't have known it if you saw him; he used to come into town wearing an old white mac and a black beret and would sometimes sleep above the works.

We moved from Lyndhurst Street to a yard at Mersey Weaver Wharf which we sold to Steelite and then to Barker's Garage at Sneyd Hill. We ran as many as fifty vehicles: ERFs, Seddons, Atkinsons and Fords. We had a lot of good drivers including Harry Kelly (CB handle Dead City Ghost) who did over twenty years for us, Harry Shepherd, Bill Schofield, Sid Condliffe, Freddie Williams, Dave Butcher (CB Red Knight), Ern 'Pep' Peppiatt, Terry Wright, Johnny Pie, Freddie Middleton, Melvyn Lofthouse, Harry Wright, Stevie Hancock, Gary Jennings, Jeff Slater, John Rowley, and Joe 'Double Top' Salt.

Then there were the members of the family who drove including Roy, Ernie (CB Red Echo) and myself (CB Red Rider) and cousins George 'Knocker' and Les. When Mountford Bros finished Dad bought 35 of their trailers and 2 Volvo tractor units and Jack Hartley, their transport manager, came to work for us. We took on all their steel work and Jack stayed with us until he passed away. We decided to sell up in 1989 and I went into partnership with Dave Butcher doing general haulage for Webbers and British Steel. I carried on working until I was seventy. We're all retired now.

George Alcock (Uncle George) - we're not sure what the vehicle is but think it's pre-1925.

George Alcock again with what had been an ambulance in WW1. This vehicle belonged to Maddocks. It had a leather clutch so when it came to a bank the driver had to stop to change gear or it would have broken the half-shafts.

This picture was taken at the depot at Mersey Weaver Wharf 45 years of Service to Industry, c1976.
L-R: Reg Alcock, cousin Knock, Terry Wright, Young George Alcock, Fred Williams, Roy Alcock and Les Alcock.

Reg has very sportingly let me include these two. The top picture shows his ERF toppling over at Platts Tiles, Tunstall. It was loaded with clay from Kingsley that had dried and was stuck in the body. Ron Joynson (owner/driver) on the left with Reg leaning against the cab. Late 1970s.

LEFT & BELOW
Derek Breeze was driving past Checkley Café in an AEC loaded with pig iron when a bus pulled out in front of him. Fitted with Westinghouse brakes, the steering locked causing him to skid on the forecourt of the café and over she went. Luckily, nobody was hurt. c1965.

Taken at Erith Docks. 16 vehicles delivering pig iron had to come back empty so piggy-backed home to save diesel. It was probably 1955, at the time of the Suez crisis. Here a Dodge is on the back of an ERF. 'Knock' is nearest the camera with the hat and George Hudd is walking towards him.

We're not sure what the occasion was but Ernie is in the cab with L-R: Les Alcock, Knocker, Jack Hartley and Ernest Peppiatt.
All photographs Alcock Collection

PAUL DULSON

My earliest recollection of riding in a lorry is in a Foden that my dad, Joe Dulson, drove. He was driving for Leese's of Shelton and it was the first brand new truck he had. My grandad worked for Leese's doing coal and corn and had got him this job because he'd been working in the pit and didn't like it. Grandad also drove a lime spreader so he did three really dirty jobs: he was exposed to dust from the corn, filthy black dust from the coal and white lime. Anyway, Dad had this Foden in about 1956 and kept it for ages.

I was born in Abbott's Road, Abbey Hulton and I can remember my mum lifting me on the table so I could look through the window to watch my dad coming down the road in his lorry. He'd pick us up and we'd go doing farm deliveries all over the place. He'd sit me on the bonnet and there used to be a rubber grommet on them then and he'd say to me 'press that.' so when it started I thought I'd done it. Anyway, that's how I got the transport bug. When he took me to the yard I'd be looking at all the other vehicles and I started wanting to go in them as well. I remember his best mate, Arthur Simpkin, let me have a ride in his sometimes.

One day when I was at the infants' school the teacher was teaching us the Lord's Prayer. We all had to go to the front, one by one, to recite it and it came to my turn. I started off OK then all of a sudden I hear this lorry and I look through the window and it's my dad going past. One minute I'm saying 'give us this day our daily bread....' and the next I'm saying 'C Leese & Sons, Corn Merchants, Pynest Street, Shelton! It was all that was in my head.

He left there and went to work for Thorley's when they were small and based in College Road. He had a brand new truck that had my mum's name 'Sheila' on the front. He started on distance work for Les McCann.

When Dad finished for Thorley's he went to Alan Clowes at Cheddleton on tippers; he had a brand new Thames Trader. This would be about 1962/63. On Sundays he'd go and load up so he was ready to go on Monday because he was paid by the load, as all the drivers were in those days. There would be me, my two cousins and my mum all riding with him. It was the time they were building the M6. We kids would climb into the body and we'd be waving to everybody as we were going up Bentilee. When we came back we'd be crammed in the cab because he'd got the load on. He'd go up there, load himself, weigh himself, write his own note out and off he'd go. Talk about trust; you couldn't do it today! When a new wagon came in we'd go up the farm to see it and mum would have a cup of tea with Alan's wife and we'd go and look at the pigs or wash the wagons off. In those days they used diesel to wash the lorries and we'd be covered in it.

After that Dad had a go at buying his own truck working for Bartholomew's on the Cement Works at Longton. It didn't last long so he tried bus driving. A lot of drivers did bus driving as 'foreigners' in those days. Anyway, he got the driving bug again and went for Dicksons of Hanley. He started on a four wheeler doing farm deliveries and this is when I was with him all the time. The teachers at school and Mr Lawton, the School Board man, knew what I was up to. I can remember when I was in the third year at Carmountside (on one of the rare occasions I was there) that 'JJ' Williams had me in front of the class showing him the places I'd been. I pointed out Hadrian's Wall where we'd run alongside it on the 66 and showed him different places on the map. I was saying 'Been there and there and slept there'. He asked me 'Where do you sleep?' I said 'Over the bonnet.' 'Isn't it cold?' 'No, it's what everybody does.'

When I got to about fourteen Dad had me unloading because you'd get to the farms and the farmers would never help. They'd say 'I want it there, see you later.' You'd have to climb on the back, drag hundredweight bags to the side and then carry to where they said. If you didn't put it where they wanted you'd be in trouble. Anyway, my old man got me carrying the bags to the side. The half hundredweights I could carry myself and I felt great I'd got a boiler suit and everything! I could rope and sheet; I could do a hitch and fasten it up by the time I was ten. I worked hard and I enjoyed it. Later Dad got promoted to the six wheeler Bedford doing all the fetching in from the main millers and the docks. I'd go with him to Joseph Rank's or Kelloggs; we'd be up at 3.00 am to get in the queue. He'd load on his own - all handball - a full 12 to 15 ton in bags. Then he'd rope and sheet and when we got back to the yard he'd have get it all off again. Then we'd go back to Manchester to CWS at Trafford Park and do it again. Sometimes we'd go to Scotland and handball peat or sugar beet pulp. Long hours and very hard work! Bob Green, who was the manager, would have me working in the warehouse sometimes, unloading the wagons. Or I'd do some washing off. When they bought a new lorry he'd say 'Ere, paint us these wheels.' And they paid me! I was the highest paid school kid on 'The Abbey' because I was on fifteen quid a week. When you think that my first job, for how long it lasted, was only paying £6.

Anyway, when Dad left there he didn't have a job to go to. We went up Hanley on the Saturday to get the meat as usual and Dad says 'We'll ring Kettle's up, our youth.' So we rang them from the phone box on Hanley Bus Station and walked down to Shelton because we didn't have a car. None of the drivers had cars in those days; they'd use their trucks to go home in. Anyway, we went down to Kettle's and Dad went in the office while I waited outside. A few minutes later he came out with a bloke named Pete who took us out for a test drive. Yes, I even went on the test. Anyway, he went back in the office when we got back and Bernard Kettle set him on. He worked there for about twenty years. There were some characters on there: Alfie Brown; a guy named Sonny, young Ian in the garage who still works there, Kenny Marrer, the late Ray Jane, and Woody. Whenever there was a big hole to be dug Kettle's were there. Actually, when I was at Mountford's and the steel strike was on Bernard Kettle gave me a job driving a tipper for him for the duration of the strike - about three months - and I loved it.

Throughout my childhood my ambition was to drive for Mountford's. I'd go down to Mountford's yard from a young age and I'd wash the odd wagon down, clean the cabs out and now and again they'd let me have a ride round the yard.

When I came to leave school I tried to get a job as an apprentice mechanic. I tried Beech's and Mountford's but wasn't successful. All I had in my head was trucks. In art lessons I'd draw trucks and when I came home I'd have all these Dinky toys painted the same colour and all lined up! Anyway, I had to get a job at TC Wild's as a mould maker and lasted a day. The bloke trying to teach me said 'Look, you're not taking any notice.' and I said 'You're dead right, mate' and picked this bucket up with the plaster in and slung it at him. He said, 'Get off or I'll get the police.' I knew my old man would kill me so I walked all the way down Longton and up Vickie Road and went to the Careers Office. They told me about a job as a Driver's Mate for S D Taylor in Huntbach Street. Taylor's sold furniture and was one of the leading credit companies. They had a 'club man' who went round and people would buy a first aid kit and pay a few pence a week and if they were a good payer they could have a record player or something - probably costing something like £50 and pay about 10 shillings a week. Taylor's went everywhere, as far up as the Lake District and in to Wales. Anyway, they set me on and I'm in this old truck with a bloke named Harry and I thought what a miserable sod he was but when I got to know him he was a laugh. There was him and Stuart in these two vans and they were both as mad as a box of frogs! I went everywhere with Harry in this BMC furniture van; it was a draughty old thing.

Joe Dulson's first new vehicle when he was driving for Leese's. Pictured at Boalloy, Congleton. 1956

I passed my car test while I was at Taylor's; I'd had lessons with Rutter's in Hanley and passed first time. There was a lad who lived across the road from me, David Cobby whose dad worked for Beresford's. Me and Dave hit it off straight away because we were both truck mad and we grew up wondering which of us would get a truck first. Well, he passed his test first because he's 12 months older than me and he got a driving job. I was still a driver's mate. I remember seeing this old crate of a truck outside my mum's house one day and thinking... that's Cobby's, that is.

I left Taylor's and went to work for Broadway House Furnishers as a driver. I'd got a better wagon than Cobby now, a $7^1/2$ ton Bedford. I remember very clearly going home in this van and how proud I was. I gave Dad a ride around the estate in it; the look on his face said it all.

Then I went to work for Dennis James and started on distance at 18. That's when I met Norman Harding; I learnt my trade from him and men like John Belfield. When I passed my Class 1, Dennis bought a brand new Leyland Boxer and I was doing all round London with about 20 drops around the West End and I was going to Scotland. It was a good job and I learnt a lot. Whenever you were in London you headed for Tooley Street Lorry Park and there I'd meet up with Dave Cobby who was on Wass's and we'd go out in the East End pubs with all our heroes: Dave Scarlett, George Palin, Barry Mcloy, Jim Alcock, Ken Kirkham, Derek Barker, Ray Kinsey and Jeff Stubbs to name but a few.

A friend of mine, Bob Edwards, drove an artic for Tipton Steel and he used to let me have a go at driving his truck whenever I was on holiday and I went with him to Preston Docks every Saturday. Consequently, I only needed about five tidy-up lessons from Ray Bourne to pass my Class 1. This saved me a lot of money.

Everyone knew I wanted to work for Mountford's and as soon as I passed I was on the phone to them every day. In the end I would say 'Hello Jack' and he'd say 'we've got nowt at the moment son, but we'll keep thee in mind.' One day I rang Jack up and he said 'Is that thay again, Duls? Thayst better come down an' let the old man have a look at thee.' I jumped in my dad's car and raced down to their yard and there's Jack Hartley standing with his hands on his hips 'Thayst got some persistence. If thayt half as good as thar old man thayt be owrate!'

So Arthur is sitting in the office and Jack says 'This is 'im that keeps ringin' up.' Anyway, John Breed was the first one in the yard that day in this big Volvo and he takes me out to see if I was OK. I was that excited I can even remember what I was wearing: a black jumper, a white Ben Sherman shirt and a pair of Levis. I looked right keen. I got in this Volvo and thought.... if any women can see me now. Actually, before that I was thinking.... If Dave Cobby could see me now he'd break his heart! He was still driving an old ERF at this time. So I did a test drive with 20 ton of steel on and I went out of Mountford's yard, across Woolliscroft Road, up round Bentilee and back in again. They say the longer the load, the easier it is. It was good; I never even hit a kerb. I said to John 'I can't believe it, I've got one.' and he said 'Well, you wunner be 'avin this one!'

When we got back he told Jack 'He's owrate.' and Jack told me I could start. I was over the moon; I could have cried. For anyone young like me to get on there it was really good. I never looked back. If Mountford's was still going I think I'd be there now.

On my first day there were two trailers for MOT to Swynnerton. Robert Hurst was in the garage and he gave me this ERF, AEH 806H; it was an ex-Thorley's that they'd bought off Les McCann and Turner's ended up buying it off Mountford's. The first time I went home in it Dad was on holiday so I went round the estate like before but this time with my younger brother John. The next day I went on the railway job running from Longport Goods Yard to BRC at Stafford. After that I did my first long load, a 45 footer with a trombone trailer. I was at Mountfords from when I was 21 in 1978 until they closed in 1982.

The experience I got while I was there: you'd do long loads, tippers, tankers, flat loads, roping and sheeting, chains, low loader work. They'd shut motorways off when we were on hire to Longton Crane Hire when we'd be moving bridges with 60 ft beams on and stuff like that. I was only 21. Every day was an adventure.

Then they bought a tipper trailer just at the time the M67 was being built, the Denton bypass, so I was doing three a day out of United Gravel to Denton in this old Seddon. It didn't half go; it would do about 63 mph but it would go up a bank that quick as well. There were some heroes up there: Barry Belfield, Alan from Tideswells and Pete off B & S. CB radio was just coming out and the fun we had. I was Wild Thing; I had it written on the truck. Then Mountford's bought an F10 from Dave Unwin which was ex-Comart. With me being next in line for the 'new' truck I thought... I've arrived! Then Jack came and put his arm around me and said 'Listen, son, we conner put a big F10 on the tipper job so our Billy's havin' that but the good news is

1978 Volvo F10 sleeper cab, ex Comart.
Mountford Bros bought this from Dave Unwin.

you can have his F88 6 wheel tractor unit.' This was his 'pride of the fleet' and what a motor!

One of the first Volvos Mountfords bought Paul had this for a while.

BELOW
Paul (left) aged 17 with driver's mate, Eric Hall. This was taken a week after he passed his test. .

ABOVE
Paul's first vehicle when he started at Mountford Bros. Alan Sturge remembers seeing him come on to Shelton Bar when he'd just started, driving this

LEFT
Paul caught napping at Rainbow Café, Derby. Dean Stevenson took the picture.

The Friday Mountford's finished Jack Hartley came and said 'Duls, Billy Poole's been on the phone and wants you to ring him.' So I did and he said 'Can you do us a flier tomorrow? East Grinstead, tip, load Redhill and back to Stoke.' This was before the M25 was built. 'Go about two o clock and I'll give you thirty quid.' So I came home and said to our youth 'We're truckin' tomorrow in Billy Poole's new motor.' So, off we went in his brand new Seddon Atki 401. Then on the Monday I went to work for Turner's and the first bloody wagon I had was the first one I'd had on Mountford's, AEH 806H! I said 'What a comedown after my big posh Volvo.' It was work, though. One day I was coming down the motorway in it and a lad we used to call Chickenbone, and Chris Clacher off Shirley's, must have been on the CB and came up alongside and said, 'You'll never guess who's in this old shed.' And they were blocking me in and I was trying to hide my

face! Anyway, I finished on Turner's and the two blokes who ran it, both named Jeff, were really nice and said I could go back any time.

I went to Webb's and I was driving EGS 515T, a Seddon Atkinson with a 250 Cummins, doing chlorine gas out of BP at Sandbach and delivering electric and gas meter boxes to power boards across the country for ERF Plastics at Biddulph Moor.

Paul had this after Bill Hartley.

Paul drove this for 10 years with only
one clutch replacement when the engine was rebuilt.

Webb's had the JR Hill contract and I had a good relationship with Mr Hill. I persuaded him to have 'EGS' painted in Hill's colours (even though it was still Webb's) to bring more work in. When Webb's closed down Harrison's of Milton bought 'EGS' expecting to get Hills's work but Mr Hill said 'only if Paul is doing it' so I ran the same truck for 10 years!

In 1992 I went to work for a firm called Smith's of Bedford. I saw the job advertised and fancied a change. They needed someone able to do paperwork and work on their own initiative and I got the job I think it was partly to do with the fact that I was the only driver who turned up in a suit. It was the best job I ever had. They sent me on a few courses and I ended up being the area team leader; I was still driving but now I had a briefcase in the cab! They sent me on a lot of courses - they were very customer focused, and this is how I came to get involved in training.

I took voluntary redundancy from Smith's and did a couple of years on Davey's before eventually applying for a job at Sainsbury's. I have been their Driver Trainer for the last ten years and for the last two we've won Sainsbury's Driver of the Year!

After Paul had left Harrisons and went to Smiths he'd pop down to wash his vehicle off in Harrisons yard. 'Milton Maid' in the centre was driven by Dave Cobby at one time.

MIDDLE: Paul with just a small selection of his 1700 models which he has either made himself, painted or collected.

BELOW:
Paul (right) with Lucy Harding (whose family owned and ran Belfield Road Services) and Alan Sturge. Now all working for Sainsbury's.

Paul with his dad, Joe. This picture was taken about nine years ago when Alan Sturge arranged a day at Trentham Gravel Quarry for the old drivers. It was a surprise for Joe and an even bigger one when he got to drive one of the vehicles.

LEFT:
Joe Dulson being taken on his final journey. Alan Sturge drove with Paul and brother, John also in the cab. Paul: 'We wanted to take him on a lorry for his final journey as he had taken us on our first one. A proper way to go.'

John and Paul down at the garage on a Saturday getting everything ship-shape for the week ahead.

Unless otherwise stated, all photos Paul Dulson Collection.

MOUNTFORD BROS. - John Breed

I grew up in Bucknall just up the road from Mountford's. Mrs Corden, the secretary at Mountford's, lived across the road from us and I always called her Auntie Rene. I started to go to the garage with her when I was nine because she used to do the wages and had to go down every week. She'd take a little white postcard with the names of the drivers on and ask them how many hours that particular week. Then she'd go home and make up the wages. As things progressed I'd go down with the card for her and then I got to washing off the lorries and filling them up and greasing on a Saturday morning. So I started, really, for Mountford's when I was nine years old in 1954.

A Mountford Bros Guy 'B' bus. Reg EH 9754, new in 1927. Mountfords also had a vehicle that was part-time lorry and part-time bus; they'd remove/add the seats and canopy as required! *Graham Potts Collection*

I remember when it was term time my mother had to virtually throw a bucket of water over me to get me out of bed but when it was the school holidays I'd be up at half past three in a morning to go to Liverpool Docks with one of the drivers. I used to go with Ronnie Chadwick, Bernard Beebe, Arthur Hill, Albert Wild or George Simmonds. At that time they had 14 lorries and about 30 trailers - from a short 20 ft that we called a bouncer, to the big extending trailers that opened up to 60ft long. Then there was the eight wheeler with what we called a bogey, like a dolly, that you could have any length of load on. The longest load we ever had on was 100ft long - it was a big steel pipe girder that went down to the Isle of Dogs.

At 12 I learnt to drive. I got promoted from filling-up to parking-up one day when Alf Shufflebotham drew on with a little Bedford tipper and said 'Well, you might as well park it now.' I said, 'I don't know how to drive that, Alf.' 'Get in, I'll show you.' He stood on the running board and I got in the driver's seat and I reversed up the yard.

At fifteen I started on a proper basis; I left school on the Friday and started working the next day. The bosses were Arthur and Freddie Mountford, two brothers. They used to call Arthur 'Cherry' and Freddie 'Freddie One Match' because he'd strike a match to light up a Senior Service in the morning and never strike another one because the next cigarette was lit with the tab of the last one.

The brothers were really good to work for; I called them Uncle Arthur and Uncle Fred. Everybody wanted to work for Mountford's it was such a good firm. I worked in the garage as a trainee mechanic with Stan Prince until I was seventeen. Stan didn't have any paper qualifications but he could make an engine talk. When we had nothing to do in the garage we'd recondition a gear box or an engine so if a lorry came in with an engine problem we'd take it out and put another one in. One day we were a bit bored and got an old chassis from up in the field and built a Bedford artic unit out of what we'd got in the garage. The only thing new that we put in was a Bedford cab.

My first job every morning was to wash all the spanners and hang them up in the cabinet. It had to be spotless for when Stan came in, because if it wasn't he'd hit me with the brush. We had a big pot-bellied stove in the garage that we'd put coke on - Mountford's had a coal business as well - and in winter they'd send me to the top of the yard with a barrow with spanners in and brake shoes to reline brakes on trailers. Some of the trailers were that long they couldn't get them in the garage so it was my job to go up in the snow doing these jobs and I'd be freezing cold. Sometimes I'd go down for a warm by the stove and they'd say, 'What are you doing down here? Get out there!' and I'd have to go back.

When I was about fourteen I went to Liverpool Docks with one of the drivers. The dockers at Liverpool were on piece work - the quicker they worked the quicker they could go home. Anyway, this particular day there's a ship from Australia or New Zealand carrying margarine being unloaded on to the quayside. Suddenly a crate falls off and splatters margarine all over the place. Seconds later this docker comes racing out on a forklift truck and hits this margarine. Well, he's skating all over the place, round and round this forklift's going. Then the driver leaps off just as this forklift goes over the side into the water. Anyway, the Mersey Dock and Harbour Board send for a diver and he's there with his big heavy lead boots on and the headgear with the window at the front and they hook him on to the crane and lower him into the water so he can attach the hook to the forklift. A short while later the forklift's being raised out of the water with the diver sitting in the driver's seat!

It used to be my job at the docks when we were sitting at the quay in the queue to draw the lorry up while the driver went to have his notes stamped in the checker's cabin. There was this old Sentinel steam truck in front one day, I'd be about thirteen, and you weren't allowed to overtake the vehicle in front. So I'm sitting there and the driver, Ronnie Chadwick, walks back with the driver of the steam lorry. Johnny says 'Why haven't you moved up, John?' I said 'Well, this steam lorry's in front.' So the steam driver says to me 'Why didn't you move it up?' 'I don't know how to drive that.' Then he says, 'Get in and I'll show you.' So I climb in this Sentinel and I can see it now, there was this big boiler in the middle with a fire going and a shovel on top with bacon and eggs frying on it! This driver says, 'Just turn this tap here and pull the lever there' and we were off and if he hadn't told me how to stop we'd have kept going until we ran out of coal. Then, of course, I had to walk all the way back to fetch the other lorry up.

When I passed my test I was in a Bedford Dormobile. I remember it was a nice summer's day and this Bedford had sliding doors on and the examiner, Dennis Church, said 'We'll leave the doors open.' So off we go and he said to me, 'Now when you get up to 30 mph I want you to stop as if somebody has run out in front of you.' Well, the catch on the door wasn't working properly on this vehicle and when I did the emergency stop the sliding door came forward at about 50mph! Dennis went white; if he'd had his hand there it would have been sliced off. One of his idiosyncrasies was to get an egg and a little piece of wood that he would use when he tested a hill start. He'd get out and place the egg behind one of the the wheels with the piece of wood behind it to stop it rolling away. Then when you did the hill start you had to do it without breaking the egg.

When I passed my test Uncle Arthur bought a little ex-army two ton tipper that I drove until I went onto the five ton Bedford. After that I went working down the gas works at Etruria on hire to William Press of Kingswinsford. They wanted a short wheel base lorry to carry 60ft pipes to get round the works so Arthur bought a little ERF. I painted it in the company colours while I was there. It had a bolster at the front and back so the pipes could go over the back of the cab and I used to weave my way through the works. The pipes are still there to this day.

When I was 20 I came in one day and the ERF had a problem so they sent me out on an Atkinson artic unit with a dolly on the back. We were carrying 60 ft railway lines. Bernard was the driver and we went to Partington Gas Works. On the way there I'd bought 'Titbits' magazine and we were sitting in the layby and in the centre spread there were pictures of cars that had gone through hedges and overturned lorries. I remember saying 'How do things like this happen, Bernard?' and he said 'Oh, they lose concentration or fall asleep.' Two hours later we were upside down in a field on this Partington site. As we had driven on to the site we were up to the axles in sludge so Bernard said, 'We'll disconnect the brake pipes and wrap 'em all up to save 'em getting covered in sludge.' As we started off along this made-up road I looked through the back window and said 'The bogey's crabbing!' As he stopped it was right on the edge of this road and the road collapsed. The bogey twisted itself and flirted the cab over like a conker on a piece of string.

We were both still in the cab when I came to and I shouted (with a bit of language) 'Get your foot off me head, Bernard!' He shouted back 'It isn't my foot.' Then some workmen came and pulled him out and when they came round to my side I said 'Well, whose foot is on my head?' The only thing I could move at the time was my left hand; my right hand was trapped, my right leg was trapped and the seat I'd been sitting on was on my chest. When I put my hand up I realised it was actually my foot on my forehead.

The workmen got a caterpillar D8 bulldozer and lifted the cab up and pulled me out. They put me in the site agent's big Zephyr and raced off down the main road with me in the back seat in my overalls and size 12 wellingtons. When they saw the ambulance coming the other way with the bell ringing they were so keen to stop it they forgot to put the handbrake on the car when they got out. There I am in this car and it's inching down the road and I'm shouting and bawling. Anyway, they managed to jump in and stop it and I was put on to a stretcher and taken to hospital in the ambulance.

I'd broken two bones in my right hand, broken my right ankle, broken three lumbar vertebrae in my spine and stretched a nerve in my left leg by 9 inches. The doctor said by the time I'm seventy I should have a good foot - apparently a nerve goes back 3cm every twelve months. Actually, my foot has started to warm up now and I can move it a bit. I should have got married the year of the accident but I got a reprieve - we married a year later! I was off work for twelve months. My mum was obviously very upset when I had the accident and when I got married she gave me a packet of cigarettes that I'd had in my pocket when it happened, it had blood on and everything.

When I was 21 I started on the artics on a Seddon. Mountford's had the first Volvos in Stoke and I eventually had one when Ronnie Chadwick said 'I think it's time John Breed had a new one.' That was the only brand new lorry I ever drove, WVT 635L. I put a radio in and I could actually hear it when the engine was running. I remember being on Shelton Bar and a chap named Alf off Bassett's, who drove a Mickey Mouse Foden, came across to look at it. He got in and turned the engine on and the wireless was on and I said 'Have you got a radio in yours, Alf?' He said, 'You could put Foden's Motorworks Band in mine and you wouldn't hear it!'

I stayed with Mountford's until they closed down; I'd been with them for 22 years full-time and from when I was nine until fifteen as a part-timer. I was out of work for three weeks and I got

ABOVE
Bernard Beebe had this accident in Neath, South Wales. The load slipped and a girder came through the back of the cab pushing him through the windscreen. He was rolling over in front of the vehicle when it turned over. Luckily, he escaped with only minor injuries.

LEFT
The cab with the girder that pushed Bernard through the windscreen.

Taking down the railway bridge from the old Stoke on Trent loop line in 1970. Mountfords got the job of moving it a few yards so the scrap men could cut it up. Note the passing traffic! The man in the donkey jacket with back to the camera is Wilf Drakeford, Mountford's driver.

Taken on a building site c 1960.
Driver Bill Hartley

RIGHT
The 100 ft load from Copestick
and Farrell in Victoria Road,
Fenton.   Not very clear pictures
but Bill Hartley, with the help of
John standing on the bogey, had
the necessary skill to get it out.
A team effort. The Volvo 240
F88 was one of the first made.

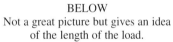

LEFT
John on the bogey.

BELOW
Not a great picture but gives an idea
of the length of the load.

Mountfords yard 1970s. Scammell 8 wheeler.

Shelton Bar Constructional
Department again 1960

Shelton Bar Constructional Department
1970s. Volvo F88.

a job on Baker's Coaches. When I was on Mountford's I used to think Leeds was a long way but since I've been with Bakers, Paris is local.

Arthur Mountford was so inoffensive; he would never want to sack anyone. If you did something wrong he'd give you a second chance. I remember he used to say 'If you feel tired, son, park up and have a sleep. We can get a new wagon; we can't get a new you.' Firms don't say that nowadays, do they.

Mountfords yard two Volvo F88 tractor units. BAC was one of the first to come into the country.

ABOVE
Shelton Bar Constructional Department 1970s Driver Bill Hartley

LEFT
Retirement! John's son had this banner made for him on his retirement from Baker's Coaches after twenty-five years.
Ros Unwin

Unless otherwise stated, all photos John Breed Collection

GORDONS TRANSPORT Alan Gordon

My Dad, Bert Gordon set up the business with money he'd saved while he was serving in the army during the war. He had a really good singing voice and whenever he went out people would buy him drinks to sing for them, so he managed to put away enough to buy his first wagon, a Bedford. His first depot was in Gower Street, Longton but he later moved to Sutherland Road.

We had thirty two Thames Traders at one time, mainly Ford D series and three artic flats running out of Mellor Mills carrying silica sand in bags. We also did vermiculite for them; I remember we used to have to pile this stuff sky-high just to get about two tons on. We also did sand and gravel out of the quarries. One of the drivers, Billy Mills used to take me out with him when I was still at school. Another driver I remember was Stan Riley; Stan used to go in the office when we were short staffed. At some stage Dad bought Suttons of Mow Cop just to get the licences and obviously took the staff on too. Tommy Johnson was their mechanic who stayed with us, and one of their drivers I remember was Freddie Woolrich.

I went to work in the business driving a Transit van and later a four wheeler with a Cummins V8, ex-BIS. I remember when we took silica sand in big containers to Ford's of Dagenham (a two-day run in those days) in 825 LVT and the workers came out to look at it because they'd never seen a twin-steer Thames Trader before. Some of the other drivers I remember working for us are Barry Carding, Ken Rushton and Tut Whalley. Mum closed the business in the late 60s after dad died.

I now work for Sainsbury's but was driving for Interlift at Chesterton doing abnormal loads until the 1990s and before that for NCB at Berry Hill moving heavy plant and equipment.

Ford Trader four wheeler

Dodge Kew with trailing axle, Billy Mills is the driver. Over the name board was written 'Cheshire Monarch'.

Thames Trader

The vehicle in the foreground was their first twin steer Thames Trader. It had a primrose conversion. Alan remembers delivering silica sand to Fords, Dagenham and people came out of the factory to look at it as they hadn't seen one before. Graham Atkinson remembers driving this on tramp work. Ken Rushton drove it before him.

LEFT
On the right is a BMC alongside Thames Traders

LEFT
A couple of Dodges and a BMC among these Thames Traders

In this line-up the first three are Thames Traders, the fourth is a Leyland Super Comet that Jack Davis drove and next to it is a 6-wheel Leyland followed by a couple more Traders and a Dodge.

Ford D Series with four in line trailer - only 26ft. Purchased from Salmon and Jones. Barry Carding drove this before going on to a Leyland.

LONG DISTANCE OR LOCAL	Telephone : STOKE-ON-TRENT 33035-6
TIPPERS OR FLAT WAGONS	**GORDON'S TRANSPORT**
SERVICES TO ALL PARTS OF THE UNITED KINGDOM	Sutherland Road, LONGTON Stoke-on-Trent, Staffs.
	Presented by

Business Card before it became C & L Gordon Ltd.

A Commer with a Perkins. Alan remembers the Ministry kept pulling this up for being overloaded on the back axle so he and his cousin shortened it by 18" on the back.

Gordons used to move garden seats and trellis work for Shentons, Uttoxeter Road.

This train had to be taken from Whaley Bridge to The Garden Festival in Stoke by the NCB and Alan got the gig. Picture taken at Whaley Bridge where a 45 ton crane had to put it on the trailer. Later, this engine went to Chatterley Whitfield and then to Foxfield.

BELOW:
This Interlift DAF was plated for 150 tons and 75 ft long. The first axle on the trailer was dead and the five behind steered. It had a donkey engine on the back of the trailer for independent steering.

This was plated for 85 tons. Scammell with a Leyland cab and 250 Big Cam engine.
All photos Alan Gordon Collection

JENKS TRANSPORT - Howard Jenks

My dad, John Jenks was born on a smallholding at Sneyd Green which was where the Sneyd Arms is now. By the time he left school his family had bought Birches Head Farm (later sold for building) and he was working there for his father. A corn merchant from Webbs of Chester used

to call on them every so often and said they needed someone to do the transport, so Dad thought about it and decided to have a go. He bought a very old ERF and started working for them in about 1953.

At some stage he acquired a yard in Scott Lidgett Road, Longport and the business grew. It was a reasonable size when I was at school; probably seven or eight units, four or five eight wheelers and two tankers delivering road fuel. My sister, Elaine, worked in the office at this

John Jenks in the cab with Ray Owen at the front. We think this is a Leyland Badger six tonner c1930. Taken in the 1960s, the Leyland is on one of their old highway trailers.

time. Dennis Alcock was Transport Manager and Ray Owen was in the garage.

I remember a time when we had a problem with the drains at the yard. We used to carry a lot of clay and obviously had to wash the trailers off but this clay must have built up and caused a blockage. Anyway, we had to sort it out so Ray Owen goes down the yard with the rods and climbs down the manhole. In the meantime my dad tells me to pump 1000 gallons out of the canal into one of the tankers and put the pipe down the drain in the garage. When I'd done he said 'Right, let it go.' Two gallons a second coming out of this pipe and Ray's at the end of it. He came out of the manhole absolutely covered; it was spurting out just like an oil strike!

Dad was a character; you never knew what he was thinking. When he decided to sell out to Dave Unwin he didn't tell anyone; he just came in one morning and told Dennis. I remember Dave bought some wagons once and needed them fetching in so I went out in a van with some drivers to collect them. When we got there we decided to put the van on the back of one of the

eight wheelers. We couldn't get the tailboard on so we put it down the side of the van, the spare wheel down the other side and just put a rope at the back. Now we were in this old Foden with a really sharp clutch and were going up Barracks Road in Newcastle. We were just coming up to the zebra crossing and this Foden suddenly rears up and I looked back and this spare wheel was bouncing down the road, straight into the side of a Mr Kipling van.

PICTURE RIGHT: John Jenks with his wife, Joyce, 1990s. Alan Holdcroft: 'On Saturdays he'd have a sheet of paper with Trunkers and Shunters on and you'd tell him how many you'd done. A Devon was £14 and a Cornwall £18. If you did a Devon you'd get £4 for a night out and for a Cornwall you'd get two nights. With Johnny Jenks if you had a day off you were sacked. He was sound, though. I remember he used to say 'You've only got to roll off a house brick and you'll be in Aberdeen!'

Graham Atkinson

I was working for Gordons in the early sixties driving a Thames Trader twin steer, 925 LVT. It was a good little motor but there was only me who'd got the patience with it. The manager at Gordons at the time was George Lowe with Stan Riley (Big Stan) and Ken Rushton in charge when George was on holiday. Arthur Tellwright, Ray Inch, Ray Hudson who drove a six wheeler carrying stone from Buxton to Bartholomews and my brother, Ian all worked there at the same time as me. I left Gordons to go to Tommy Deggs at Stableford Transport. I had an AEC four wheeler 646 SVT when I went there and then a KC Dodge artic, JEH 905D. I left there to go to John Jenks as a shunter.

When I went to John he'd got three eight wheelers and about nine artics and I drove them all. There were no twin steers; they were all double drive tractor units because of the type of work we were on. We carried pipes for Stanton, castings for Chesterfield Pipes, asbestos for Turners, paper for Modo at Chester, bottles for Garstan and clay up from Cornwall to James Kents where it was processed and taken back down to Cornwall again. I remember we also did work for Harrison Mayer, Staffordshire Potteries and Spode. The old pot banks were designed for horses and carts not for our long vehicles - some of our tractor units were actually tipper chassis - but we managed to get in and out.

Some of the people I remember working with at Jenks's were: Peter Almond, Tony Smith, Ron Condliffe, Patrick Lunny, John McClory, Ray Taylor, Alan Mayer, George Deakin, Kenny Worthington, Joe Sykes and Alan Holdcroft. We had a chap named Brian Thomson whose nickname was 'The Trooper' and he took a St Bernard dog everywhere with him. Ray Owen was in the garage and when we came in at night Howard used to go round checking the tyres and wheel nuts. Another good lad was Mick Austin who was a shunter the same as me; he left to go to McGuinness's driving a Hiab wagon.

John Jenks's lorries must have had a good home because there are one or two still going strong - DVT 723J is still being worked as a wrecker wagon with a crane on the back. I've seen another one in Northumbria, up near Berwick on Tweed, coming out of a forest with a great load of logs on - WVT 290G. REH 589L was sold in Brindley Ford last year and has gone down Ipswich way, I believe.

I retired from my last job at Severn Trent in 2000.

Note: Dave Unwin - I remember selling REH 589L to Billy Taylor. Billy built and fitted the wrecking equipment to it and did such a good job that he sold it to Reliance Garages, the main ERF dealers in Yorkshire. He then bought another twin steer of Jenks's YKB 135J and did the same conversion on that. He built them in our workshop at Checkley; he was a brilliant engineer.

Mick Austin

I was working for Don Smith before I went to Jenks's. I was the last one driving an eight wheeler for John Jenks. I remember I came in the yard one Saturday morning and John told me to park up and go and see him in his office. I didn't know what was going on; I thought I was finishing. Anyway, he told me to go to Bassetts at 8.00 am on the following Monday. I thought he'd got me a job there but he said 'You go for your test next Friday.' So that's how I got my class 1. There are a couple of drivers not mentioned above that I remember: Terry Snape and Mick Jackson who were both good lads.

This was taken in the 1950s on the farm at Birches Head.

BELOW
We don't know anything about this picture if you do, then Howard would love to hear from you.

NEH 493E which Barry Almond drove.
All photos Howard Jenks Collection

PETER STEVENSON

I started in transport when I left school in 1954 working at Adams Butter in Leek. I was driver's mate to John Lancaster. I learnt to drive while I was there and when you were 21 you were eligible to drive a big vehicle. Johnny Lancaster was a lovely guy. I remember he had this Bedford and I used to go to sleep while he was driving - he used to lift the bonnet and it made such a racket.

I remember working for F V Smith of Normacot (later Comart) just doing a trunk run from Longton to Glasgow. One week you'd go all the way and stop overnight there and the following week you'd go as far as the Jungle Café and change over with a guy who'd brought one from Hamilton. One night I'd stopped at Moss just outside Carlisle. It was snowing and cold and after I'd had something to eat I set off. I was giving two lads a lift in the cab and as we got nearer to Hamilton and it was coming light, I thought there was a sheet flapping or something. I'd got a load of bricks on, so I pulled over, and it was this old tramp; he'd got on the back while I was in the Moss and climbed under the sheet at the back of the bricks. The snow was coming down and this guy was freezing cold; his face was purple! I said 'I'm not taking you any further, mate. You'd better get off and go and get warmed up or you'll be dead.' So he wandered off. I couldn't do anything else. When it's wet, the spray gets sucked back on to the vehicle. He was soaked!

After Smiths I worked for Davey Roadways; they were good days. I was driving an ERF, a very early one with an oval grill. If you went over a cat's eye you had to slow down in one of them. When I was at Davey's it was Barry who was in charge. I was coming up the road with a load of flints one day and there was nobody to help me shovel them off, so Barry said 'I'll come with you'. We used to have flatbeds with sides on so you got all your stuff on one side. I thought he wouldn't be able to do it but we started, one at each end, and he was as quick as me getting to the middle.

I went back to Adams Butter for a while and I remember Les Bailey having his accident. I wasn't there when it happened but I came across it soon after. I knew it was him, obviously. I couldn't stop because the police wouldn't let you. I went to see him at Luton and Dunstable Hospital but I only went once because it upset me. He said 'I understand if you don't want to come again.' Anyway, he recovered alright. He's a great bloke; I've only ever worked with good lads.

I finished at Adams because I'd married and needed more money so I went to Beresfords at Tunstall. My first trip was to DAF Trucks in Eindhoven one Sunday morning. Phil Bunch followed me and showed me the ropes. As time went by I'd take my wife, Sheila, and the kids with me. You'd say to Mr Dale 'OK to take the wife?' and he'd say it was and would give you a good trip to somewhere like Nice or Paris.

I once had to go to a weather station just outside Geneva to deliver equipment. There were four of us in convoy and we got to this

This picture was probably taken in Italy when Pete was delivering balers for Beresfords. *Pete Stevenson*

base camp and the bloke there had to phone up the station on top of this mountain. I think it was Mount Saleve on the border of France and Italy about 4km from Geneva. This guy came down on something like a cable car but it was just a flat bed with little sides on - just holding on as it came down this mountain side. He said 'Would you like to come up and have a look around the weather station?' So me and Johnny Pelikan went on this platform, through the clouds to the top, about 1400 metres up. When we got there he showed us all the technology, receivers and such; you could hear all the planes coming in to the airports.

One day, when I was bringing reels of paper for the Sentinel in Hanley, I turned my vehicle over. I was driving a Scania 110 and was exiting Five Ways Island at Worcester. I think the load slipped because instead of going over on to the grass verge, it went the other way. I shot through the windscreen backwards and I ended up lying on the windscreen on the grass. Unbelievably, the next vehicle to come along was the manager of Thor

Ros Unwin took this photo of Pete at Uttoxeter Show in 2012. Pete drove it at one time.

Transport in Stoke who phoned for an ambulance to take me to hospital. I injured my left thigh and had pieces of glass in my back but otherwise I was OK. It happened on January 30th I remember that because it was my birthday - and I spent the night in hospital. The next day Mick Salt, one of Beresfords drivers, came to collect me.

I remember standing in a bar in Spain once with a driver and we got arrested. At that time there was all this trouble with Baader Meinhoff and someone had phoned the police and said we looked suspicious. The police came into the bar and pushed us out at gunpoint and we had to convince them we were drivers not international terrorists!

I finished with Beresfords and went to Shirley's. I was on an ERF when I started and then a Volvo F89. Volvos were luxury - you were King of the Road! When I first went there Arthur's mum used to hold a meeting of drivers every month so they could air any grievances. If someone moaned that he wasn't getting paid as much as someone else she'd 'shoot them down' by fetching the records and showing them. I worked for Arthur for 21 years full time and still do two days a week for him. When I finished full-time they gave me a gold watch - I really appreciated that.

Pete's Volvo F10 in Wyatt livery delivering to Pedigree Pet Foods at Peterborough.
Pete Stevenson

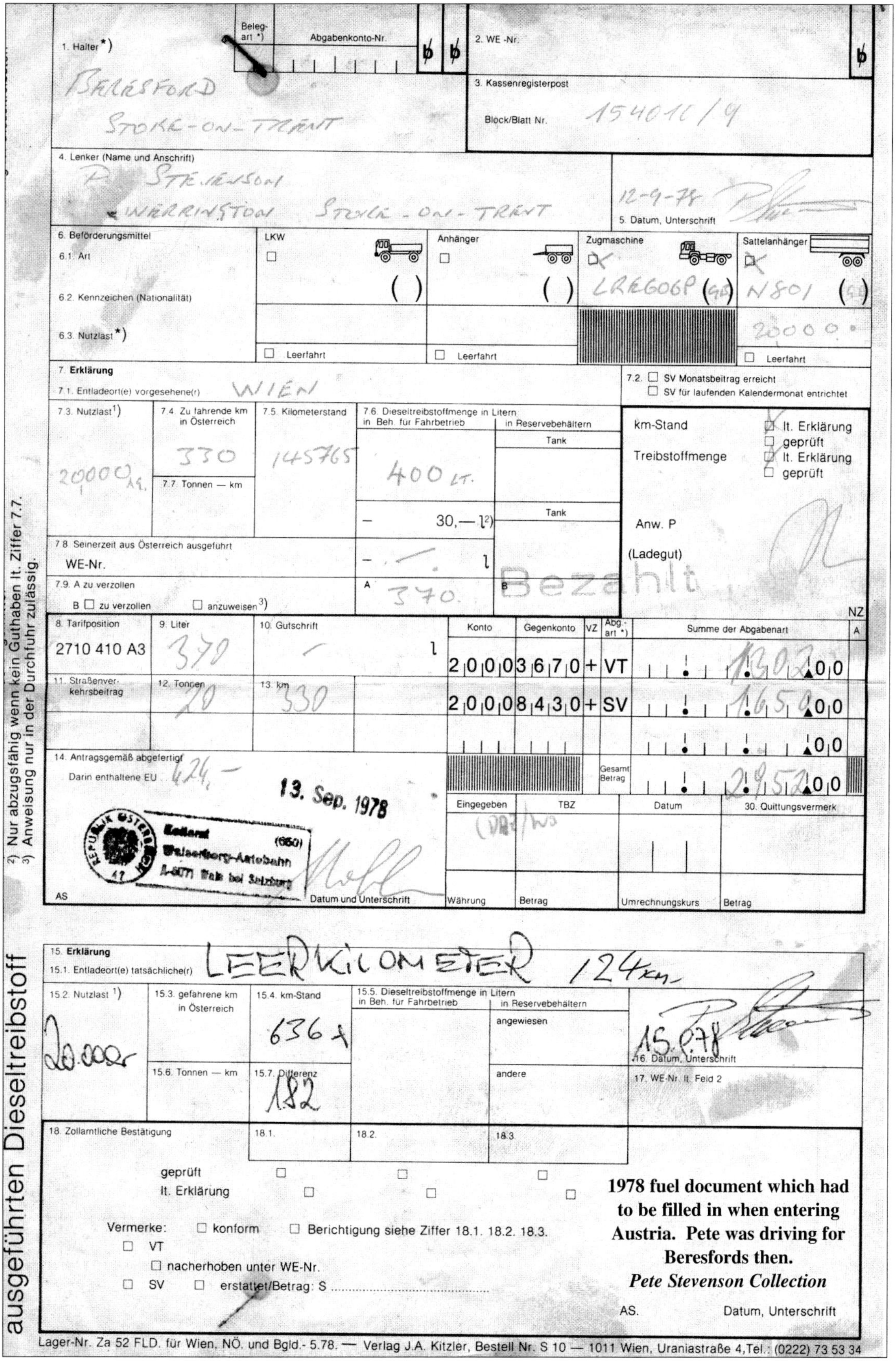

1. Halter*) BERESFORD STOKE-ON-TRENT

Beleg-art *) | Abgabenkonto-Nr. | 2. WE-Nr.

3. Kassenregisterpost Block/Blatt Nr. 154016/9

4. Lenker (Name und Anschrift) P. STEVENSON WARRINGTON STOKE-ON-TRENT

5. Datum, Unterschrift 12-9-78

6. Beförderungsmittel	LKW	Anhänger	Zugmaschine	Sattelanhänger
6.1. Art	☐	☐	☒	☒
6.2. Kennzeichen (Nationalität)	( )	( )	LRE606P (GB)	N801 (GB)
6.3. Nutzlast*)				20000
	☐ Leerfahrt	☐ Leerfahrt		☐ Leerfahrt

7. Erklärung
7.1. Entladeort(e) vorgesehene(r) WIEN
7.2. ☐ SV Monatsbeitrag erreicht ☐ SV für laufenden Kalendermonat entrichtet

7.3. Nutzlast 1)	7.4. Zu fahrende km in Österreich	7.5. Kilometerstand	7.6. Dieseltreibstoffmenge in Litern in Beh. für Fahrbetrieb	in Reservebehältern
20000 kg.	330	145765	400 LT.	Tank
	7.7. Tonnen — km		– 30,— l 2)	Tank

km-Stand ☒ lt. Erklärung ☐ geprüft
Treibstoffmenge ☒ lt. Erklärung ☐ geprüft
Anw. P (Ladegut)

7.8. Seinerzeit aus Österreich ausgeführt WE-Nr. – l
7.9. A zu verzollen B ☐ zu verzollen ☐ anzuweisen 3) A 370. B Bezahlt

8. Tarifposition	9. Liter	10. Gutschrift	Konto	Gegenkonto	VZ	Abg.-art *)	Summe der Abgabenart	NZ A
2710 410 A3	370	– l	2000	3670	+	VT	1302,00	
11. Straßenverkehrsbeitrag	12. Tonnen 20	13. km 330	2000	8430	+	SV	1650,00	
							,00	
14. Antragsgemäß abgefertigt 424,– Darin enthaltene EU						Gesamt Betrag	2952,00	

13. Sep. 1978

REPUBLIK ÖSTERREICH Zollamt (960) Walserberg-Autobahn A-5071 Wals bei Salzburg

AS Datum und Unterschrift

Eingegeben	TBZ	Datum	30. Quittungsvermerk
Währung	Betrag	Umrechnungskurs	Betrag

15. Erklärung
15.1. Entladeort(e) tatsächliche(r) LEERKILOMETER 124 km

15.2. Nutzlast 1)	15.3. gefahrene km in Österreich	15.4. km-Stand	15.5. Dieseltreibstoffmenge in Litern in Beh. für Fahrbetrieb	in Reservebehältern
20.000 kg		636 +		angewiesen
	15.6. Tonnen — km	15.7. Differenz 182		andere

16. Datum, Unterschrift 15.9.78
17. WE-Nr. lt. Feld 2

18. Zollamtliche Bestätigung | 18.1. | 18.2. | 18.3.
geprüft ☐ ☐ ☐
lt. Erklärung ☐ ☐ ☐
Vermerke: ☐ konform ☐ Berichtigung siehe Ziffer 18.1. 18.2. 18.3.
☐ VT
☐ nacherhoben unter WE-Nr.
☐ SV ☐ erstattet/Betrag: S ....
AS. Datum, Unterschrift

*) 2) Nur abzugsfähig wenn kein Guthaben lt. Ziffer 7.7.
3) Anweisung nur in der Durchfuhr zulässig.

ausgeführten Dieseltreibstoff

Lager-Nr. Za 52 FLD. für Wien, NÖ. und Bgld.- 5.78. — Verlag J.A. Kitzler, Bestell Nr. S 10 — 1011 Wien, Uraniastraße 4, Tel.: (0222) 73 53 34

1978 fuel document which had to be filled in when entering Austria. Pete was driving for Beresfords then.
Pete Stevenson Collection

M F TYLER - Karl Tyler

My dad, Malcolm Tyler, was born in 1944 in Sneyd Green. He trained as a cabinet maker but became a coal man when a relative who'd been running a coal business at Sneyd Hill, retired. Dad took over the business in 1972. He'd fetch coal from Wolstanton Colliery then bag it and deliver to regular customers. After a while he had the opportunity to work on the colliery, moving the coal around the wharf on his truck, which he did for quite a while. At some stage he started doing small bulk deliveries, so throughout most of the 1970s he was working on Wolstanton.

Taken at the yard L-R: Drew Owen, Malcolm, Karl and Gary Sherratt

Dad's first yard was in Northwood where the Co-op is now and his first employee was Brian Davies from Milton. We moved to Sneyd Hill in about 1978.

I can remember my father was always at work; I used to go to work with him on Saturday mornings from a very young age. Dad was a hard man because no matter how ill he was he'd always get on with his work. He would never complain. One morning in December 1999 he was having some pains so I rang the doctor. When I told Dad he'd have to go to the surgery he said 'Yeah, take me up.' I knew there was something seriously wrong because he would never say that. When we got to the surgery the doctor examined him and told him he'd pulled his shoulder. We came back and were getting ready to go home at lunch time and I said 'I'll go and lock up.' When I came back to the office he was on the floor. I think he was still just about with us when we got to the hospital but he died shortly afterwards. He was 54 years old. He was a big smoker and, to be honest, if he couldn't be at the depot and he couldn't smoke and run the company he would have felt that life wasn't worth living.

I was 32 then and although I worked in the business I was actually employed by PMT as a fitter. I'd do the early shift for PMT and be back here just after lunch time and, of course, I worked weekends. Dad and I fought like cat and dog. I thought he was too stuck in his ways because the job had moved on so much but he wouldn't change. I'd be saying what I thought we should be doing and he would disagree.

When I first took over after Dad died we had nine vehicles. Any transition is difficult and from an accounting point of view I didn't know much so that was particularly hard for me. Mum did the books at the time but in 2007 she was taken ill and passed away. My wife, Nicola, now works alongside me in the office.

I remember during the miners' strike that a number of hauliers came out of South Wales to work up here because the unions were very strong down there and nothing was moving. Several owner-drivers and hauliers came up and parked in this yard; they actually slept in the offices. There was plenty of room in the yard for their vehicles because Dad only had four or five at the time. They based themselves here and worked out of Hem Heath and Wolstanton. We had the police outside every night to make sure nothing untoward happened. We had no option but to work - it was the only work we did and the drivers, like the miners, were worried about their jobs.

Alan Sturge M F Tyler

When Malcolm was a coal man he used to do five tons in the morning and five in the afternoon; he was a hard worker. I remember we used to go to the Coal Merchants' Dinner and you could spot the coal men because their hands were as black as their bow ties. They were all the same, their hands would crack in winter and the coal dust would get in and they couldn't get it out. Malcolm had a Bedford TK and I remember seeing him one day, soaked to the skin and the leather coal jacket he wore looked just like a big wash leather. I said, 'You're soaking wet!' He replied, 'It's alright my skin's waterproof!' He was a grand chap, very down-to-earth.

Malcolm with a new Foden 8 wheeler, just delivered. 1980

Malcolm's coal lorry, MYG 980D

The watercolour of Malcolm's coal lorry that George Pritchard did. George was four days into his employment with Tylers when he was blown off the top of their 8 wheel ERF tipper at the Avenue Coking Plant breaking both his heels. It was while recovering at home he painted this. Karl still has the picture.
George Pritchard

RIGHT
L-R: Howard Williams who retired about six years ago, Maurice Walker (ex Nixons) and Maurice Kriehn who still works for the company.

This ERF was driven by David Calcott who still works for the company. He was taking 60 ft steel pipes from Longport Railway Station to Nottingham. Picture taken about 1989.

Some of the current fleet parked in the yard. All photos unless otherwise stated Karl Tyler Collection

R BIRKS TRANSPORT LIMITED (1954-1974) - Maurice Birks

My father, Reg Birks, was born in 1915 at Spout Cottages, Baddeley Edge. His first venture into road haulage started before the war when he drove a 3 ton Bedford for Percy Warburton of Uttoxeter. He collected churns of milk from local farmers and brought them into the town's Wilts United Dairies. Sometimes he would attach a portable container on to do furniture removals and about twice a year he would take reclaimed sack bags to Liverpool.

Warburton's Dennis Jubilant that Reg drove after the war.

At the outbreak of the second world war the Bedford was requisitioned by the army and a Leyland Octopus took its place. Under the Ministry of War Transport he regularly took plasterboards from the local factory to destinations. He was then called up and was in the Ordnance Corps. On D Day +2 he went over to France with a Diamond T tank transporter delivering and recovering tanks.

After the war he went back to Warburtons driving a Dennis Jubilant 12 tonner. This still had MWT 973/191 painted on the cab! By now one of its roles was taking export goods for Bamford Limited to Liverpool Docks and bringing cattle food back for Staffordshire Farmers at Tutbury.

I left school in 1948 and in 1949 went as mate to my father on the Dennis until nationalization claimed most of the hauliers and father became Manager of BRS at Dove Bank Garage, Uttoxeter. I did 5 years in the Fleet Air Arm until I bought myself out to help dad who, when BRS disbanded, started on his own account by purchasing a 5 ton 'O' type petrol Bedford. Shortly afterwards he bought his work-horse, a 12 ton petrol 'O' type Bedford with a 20 ft Scammell trailer. Both these were obtained with special A licences from BRS. He had a pair of skids made for the job of unloading when he started to deliver for JCB. I passed my test on the 5 ton Bedford and was carrying anything from earthenware, Marley roofing tiles, cattle food as well as raw materials into Elkes Biscuits.

Father was working day and night to make a go of it - sometimes he would even help out on the end of the assembly line at JCB to get his machine ready for loading. He'd then get a few hours sleep and set off to do the delivery. It was a case of when empty having to return straight back to pick the next machine up. At weekends he followed his old army routine of greasing all round as well as regular engine oil change and keep on top of the paperwork.

It wasn't long after I passed my test that the 'O' type 5 tonner was replaced with an 'S' type

ABOVE:
Reg and his men with Diamond
T tank recovery outfit. 1944

LEFT: Philip Mason, Maurice's
cousin, a sales rep for the
Dodge agent, Shortland Motors.

RIGHT
Maurice's parents taken at a
wedding

**Maurice's Albion and
Reg's Bedford. 1958.
Taken at the new
premises at Dove
Bank Garage,
Uttoxeter**

Bedford which was fitted with a Perkins P6 engine; a swine to start in winter. It was a case of a piece of diesel-soaked rag on a piece of wire being lit and played over the air intake as you tried to start it. I would usually park overnight at the top of a bank and roll it off to jump start. Twelve months later, after delivering a load of earthenware, I returned with a pile of loose straw which was used for packing earthenware. I took it to the local tip at a farm just out of town and was told to park alongside. I started throwing the straw off with a garden fork when all of a sudden the first lot I'd thrown off lit and the flames raced up the slope. I was in the cab with flames coming in the window trying to move the vehicle but the back axle was in a hole and I couldn't budge it. Anyway, it all went up in flames. It was a write-off and we were paid out. We purchased an Albion with a longer body and it was coach-painted and looked very imposing.

About this time we moved into an operating base at the same place where dad had been BRS manager at Dove Bank and shortly afterwards obtained two contract licences which enabled us to get rid of Dad's 'O' type artic unit and operate with three new Bedford 'S' type units as things at JCB Rocester were going like an express train and we had a job to keep pace.

We obtained an extra licence by buying an ex-army OY Bedford long wheelbase tipper from a client at Hollington who had died and they had let his business go down. I had to officially work for the family for a year to prove that there was a business to take over. I was carrying brewer's grain and Hollington stone. The Bedford was giving a lot of trouble so we exchanged it for an 8 ton ERF with a 4LK Gardner engine. The licence was eventually granted.

The beauty of delivering JCBs was that you had a quick turnaround - even at the docks - you could unload with the help of the portable ramps and within fifteen minutes you were on your way home. This came with a lot of empty running on returning home unless we brought engines back from Dagenham and Bathgate because JCBs were being produced like there was no tomorrow!

There was an amusing incident once when four of us loaded with engines stopped at a cafe in Markyate on the old A5. The bedroom was long with beds either side. My three drivers were a bit cab happy and relating different tales; the eldest was rambling on and on about an eight

Leyland Beaver. Destined for a fair in Belgium the machines are being delivered to Felixstowe Docks, 1968

wheeler. Then, all of a sudden, a driver down at the far end got out of bed and made a job of pulling it towards the middle then pulled it back again. Of course, our driver who had been telling the tale just had to ask him 'Are you alright, mate?' The reply came back, 'Oh, yes, just making room for that bloody eight wheeler to get through!'

When Mr Joe (Bamford) asked why the machines were slow in being moved and why we didn't get more vehicles, he was interested to learn about the ins and outs of the licensing system - the A and D licence application. He took Dad in his Rolls JCB1 to the next application and stood for him against the objectors - British Rail and BRS. The case was granted and we bought a Guy Invincible tractor unit and a four-in-line trailer. The Guy had a German ZF gearbox and anyone not used to it had one hell of a job engaging second gear! However, it was a great addition having a fifth wheel coupling as opposed to the automatic Scammell type that was on the Bedfords.

One basic headache was Mr Joe's policy of not letting a machine go off the bank until it was paid for. This was stuck to rigidly. We might have a vehicle waiting for a load and having to wait for the post to come in. If the cheque arrived it was all system go. The only times it wasn't followed was occasionally by arrangement when we delivered the machine but did not unload it until we had the cheque in our hands!

If we delivered in the London area or anywhere in the S/E or N/E of Fords Factory at Dagenham, provided we knew beforehand if there was enough for a load, we would run in there for a load of tractors which consisted of engine, axle and gearbox mounted on a wooden skip -like a pallet. These were placed crossways on the trailer which meant seven on a 30ft trailer. Later the total power unit, engine, axle and gearbox were changed to BMC which meant a long haul from Bathgate. This proved very testing as there was only one JCB agent in Scotland (Glasgow) and this sometimes meant running empty to Bathgate to collect a load.

Apart from the four wheeler which did general work the artics did a lot of empty running but it still made a profit to enable us to carry on buying new vehicles. It was obviously the icing on the cake if we brought the engines back as a return load. We also had quick turn-round times at each end either loading at JCB or at the delivery point.

Mr Joe, not one to miss a bit of free publicity, got us to line up the loaded vehicles at a recently installed 'first in the country' unmanned level crossing on the Rocester to Uttoxeter road at Spath. The TV news cameras and local newspaper people were all there for the official opening in February 1961.

My mother died in 1969 and Dad remarried in 1972. We were now a limited company and

AEC (left) with Dodges on Uttoxeter's lorry park.

operating with four low loaders; 30 and 40 foot flatbeds; 40 vans and TIR trailers along with a Mercedes van and a 4 wheeler. Quite a change from the humble beginnings. Dad was in hospital in 1973 and it came as no surprise when he sold up in 1974 and moved to Cornwall. Dad died in 1978

We had a great bunch of drivers who were always ready to accept the odd one or two nights out. When they had loaded and topped up with diesel, they knocked off and if there were enough of them they would play cards in the rest room until they went home.

Maurice and his wife, Ida, in 1973 at the Dinner Dance at Trentham Gardens Ballroom

Les Hitchens

When I first went to work for Reg I was given a rattle can of a Ford but when I finished I was driving a Volvo. He always tried new vehicles out on me, on the basis that if I couldn't break it nobody else could! It was a good company to work for, like one big happy family.

When Reg decided to close the firm he gave us 12 months' notice and said if any of us wanted to leave before that then they would still get their full redundancy. I think two went early out of the sixteen of us. Reg was a very honest boss; I could always work my money out every week and he knew that and he would say to me, 'Is it all right, Big Un?' He had his tantrums like everyone else but he was at a slight disadvantage because he was only small and most of his drivers were big like me. I went to work for Bamfords and eventually sat my exams and became Transport Manager. When I left there I went working on a milk round for the Co-op and eventually bought the round and worked for myself. I retired in 2000.

Jim Godsafe

When I started driving for Reg I drove a 4 wheel Dodge. One day I was on my way up the M6 to collect a load of cattle food from Liverpool when I hit a 'pea souper' of a fog. I had just overtaken a slower vehicle when I saw a black blob appear in front of me. I swerved into the fast lane and could just make out a stationary vehicle without any lights on. I pulled back over to the hard shoulder and found a telephone. I told the operator to get all the services. He asked why and I just held the phone in the air so he could hear the vehicles colliding into each other. He said 'Bloody Hell!' Apparently, there were about 70 vehicles involved. As I was walking back to see if I could help anybody I found a body on the floor. I recognised the overalls as belonging to one of our drivers. I was able to see to him; he was seriously injured and finished up in Chester Hospital. Luckily, he lived.

Another time I was on my way to do a delivery at Southampton and was approaching Gaydon RAF Station when a Triumph Vitesse overtook me and then immediately slammed his brakes on to turn into the gateway. Well, I had to stop and another lorry ran into the bucket of the JCB overhanging the rear of my trailer, trapping the driver in his cab by his legs. I borrowed a chain from the site and attached it to the bucket on the digger and freed him. The ambulance man told me that if I hadn't done this he would have died. His wife and children couldn't thank me enough when I visited the hospital to see him. The car driver was traced and was fined and banned from driving. I showed the man the picture of his lorry and he couldn't believe how he had survived.

ABOVE
P Warburton's Bedford loaded with
reusable empty corn sacks destined for
Liverpool, 1939. The vehicle was
requisitioned by the government in 1940.

ABOVE
The Christmas Dinner Dance at Trentham
Gardens Ballroom. Rear L-R: George
Kavanagh, Stuart Hitchens, Les Hitchens, Roy
Keyte and Tom Forsyth. Front L-R: Geoff
Bullock, Ron Trott, Reg, Jim Godsafe and
Maurice. 1973. *All photos M Birks Collection.*

RIGHT
Reg posing beside
his Diamond T.
1944

J K STURGE - Alan Sturge

Dad started in business in 1946 when he came out of the RAF. He worked for a while at Michelin in Stoke but wanted to be in transport so he borrowed £250 and bought his first truck - an Austin 6 wheeler. He went to work at the gravel pit at Trentham Gardens. However, the quarry was forced to close because the Local Authority claimed it was disfiguring the countryside; the motorway runs through there now. The man who had the rights to extract the gravel was Major Cornforth and he transferred from Trentham to Lordsley Quarry at Pipe Gate in 1947, but he continued to call it Trentham Gravel. Dad was there right from the beginning.

When I was two years old and my brother John was three, my mother had twins, Dianne and David. Dad was working every hour possible to earn a living. One night when he came home from work he was met at the door by Mum sobbing uncontrollably with a crying twin under each arm and John and I wrapped around each leg. She said, 'Ken, I can't manage like this!' So Dad took control of the situation, like he always did, and said 'Alright, I'll take the boys with me and you look after the twins.' At 4.30 the next morning we were bundled into his Austin truck with bottles and nappies and went to work with him almost every day until we started school. This is how I became addicted to trucks and transport. Every school holiday and probably, on reflection, most days when I should have been in school, I would be working with Dad, right up to leaving school at 15.

Dad trusted my driving skills because he'd taught me. When I was only 11 he'd pull into the quarry, stop at the canteen and get out to fill the billycan and make toast while I'd drive down to the weighbridge. I'd load with gravel or sand, back to weigh and collect delivery notes and then drive back to the canteen where Dad would take over; he would eat and drink on the road.

In 1962 I left school and went to work in the quarry with a truck my father bought for me. I'd been going there since I was young but now I was fifteen I had my own vehicle. I worked six days a week stocking the sand and received £1.50 pocket money; I never had a wage until I got married when I was 21. As I wasn't old enough to drive on the road my dad used to drop me off every morning at five o clock and I'd start working while he went out delivering all day. Sometimes he'd be late coming back and I'd be sitting there at 7.00 or 8.00 at night on my own, sometimes in the dark, waiting for him. I had no way of getting home because the quarry was a long way from where we lived in Vernon Avenue, Audley.

I can remember a firm called Gordon's Transport in Longton which was quite a big outfit. They worked out of the quarries and ran twenty-odd vehicles. I remember them running some Chinese 6 Thames Traders which came brand new from Salmon and Jones's in Longton. They were supplying all the ready mixed concrete plants with sand and gravel so when they came to the quarry they were priority - straight in and straight out again. They were as mad as March hares - Hell Drivers!

The quarry was a part of my life that I'll never forget; it's recently been demolished and thieves have broken in and started stealing what's left. I can remember the bins were made for two little wagons to go in side by side but when you look at the size of the trucks you wonder how they got in. Eight-wheelers couldn't get right under so they were loaded at the back, then the driver would have to come out, shovel the load to the front and back in again so he could get the rest of the load on. Major Cornforth's house was further up at Loggerheads and the quarry eventually reached his house so he had it demolished and continued through.

One day my dad was delivering a load of sand to the British Steelworks at Etruria to their

Alan and his brother in their father's first truck, an Austin K6. This picture taken at Trentham Gardens where the old quarry was. c1950

LEFT
Alan in the driving seat again with his dad, Ken. This is an Austin K6 again, ex war department. This was the first 6 wheeler to go into Trentham Gravel pit.

BELOW
Lordsley Quarry, Pipe Gate. The small vehicle facing on the left is the one Alan had when he was just fifteen.

concrete batching plant and bumped into an old friend, Vic Hughes who was now Clerk of the Works. He said to my dad 'So, you've got your own truck, Ken.' Dad told him he'd actually got two as I was working in the quarry and he asked Vic how much they paid. He said 'We're paying 18 shillings an hour.' At that time I was getting 10 shillings an hour for my truck so my dad asked him if he could accommodate the two of us and, if so, for how long. Vic said 'Well, we can give you three months' work.' So my dad added it up in his head and thought we could double our money in three months. So off we went to the steelworks the following morning. He had to tow me with a chain from Pipe Gate to Etruria because I was still too young to drive on the road. That was in 1964 and we stayed there until 2000!

One Friday in 1969 my dad had gone to work as usual and had a massive heart attack. I'd gone out delivering and when I got back I was told what had happened. I said 'Don't be stupid, I came in with him this morning.' Anyway, I drove over to the hospital and my eldest brother was there. Dad was asleep and he had all these wires attached to him. He died that night, he was 47. Mother was in a state; four of the five children still at home were school age. At Dad's funeral at Audley Church so many people came that some had to stand outside to listen to the service. He was a very well-known and respected gentleman who was always fun to be around.

Mother had become a partner in the firm only a few months earlier which was lucky because Dad hadn't made a will. Until his estate was settled we were allowed to operate the company but this was no easy task. My mum had a letter from the steelworks, I still have it somewhere, saying that they'd look after her sons if we continued to work there, which we did. When Dad died I was 22 and my eldest brother, John was 23. John had recently come into the business after serving his time as an engineer. When Malcolm, our younger brother left school he joined the business too and our youngest brother, Gary joined us when he was seventeen and carved out his own role within the company.

I remember when Malcolm first started at the steelworks one of his tasks was to make sure the pot was on the stove ready for the men at break time. He decided to 'automate' this job so he could get on with other things. He rigged a system with an old oil can so a squirt of oil was dispensed intermittently onto the fire. Brilliant. Unfortunately, Malc took his eye off the ball one day and when the men went for a brew the entire cabin was ablaze! It was a long time before he dared to come down from the top of the shale tip and face Dad!

After Dad died we struggled on slowly expanding the company and learning as we went along. Over the next 30 years we went from 6 trucks to 16 along with 40 trailers and a host of on-site machines at Shelton. In 1975 we bought an aggregate supply company, Gwenstan Supplies, a well-established company selling sand and gravel which fitted in with our red ash operation at the steelworks. We finished selling aggregates in the early 1990s.

At the steelworks we always worked three shifts: days, noons and nights, every day of the year. I remember one year one of the lads, a Scot named Michael, asked if he could work over the Christmas period which included New Year. I said 'Well, what about Hogmanay?' He said 'I'll not be any trouble.' Well, he was trouble. It came to New Year's Eve and he went out and sold the watch his wife had bought him for Christmas. Then he went to the pub at the end of Forge Lane and 'drank' the money he'd had for this watch. He came back, got into his dump truck and took some pig iron to the tip. When he was coming back in he forgot to lower the tipping body and took out two huge gas pipes. This was a serious problem on the steelworks as they ran on gas and it was a major shutdown. They were on to us in the middle of the night 'Get your backsides down here!' So we all went down. Anyway, in the end the insurance paid out. I

This picture was taken on a Sunday morning at the bottom of Vernon Avenue where the family lived. It's an Austin K6, Alan at the wheel!

LEFT
A family break in North Wales. Alan, John, Malcolm, Marilyn and Diane. c1956.

BELOW
The scene on a Saturday afternoon at the steelworks.

ABOVE
Again, on a Saturday
afternoon, some of Sturge's
vehicles and machinery.

ABOVE
Colleen, Alan's daughter,
setting out on her first
journey after passing her
Class 1. This was in 1996
and she was taking the
load to Peterborough.

LEFT
Colleen again, operating
one of the machines on a
Sunday morning.

Miraculously the driver of this, Ray Gilling, only suffered a broken collarbone when he was in a collision with a furniture van on the M1

BELOW
A line up of some Sturge vehicles taken at the steelworks.

In 1997 J K Sturge achieved their British Standard 5750 accreditation. This picture taken at the steelworks. L-R: Malcolm, Alan, John, Mum (Vera) and Gary.

never saw that man again - he didn't even come back for his money.

One of our burners came from Wolverhampton every day on the train. This guy would get off at Etruria and walk on to the steelworks and then go home at night on the train. His name was Reg and he worked for us for 13 years. When we finished in 2000 we decided we'd take everybody out with their wives for a real good night. I said to Reg 'Would you like to bring your wife up and have a night out with us?' My brother was there and he looked at us both and said 'You're joking aren't you? I'd sooner eat with the devil than with you pair of bastards!' I said 'But Reg, you've worked for us for thirteen years.' 'Yes, but I don't like you; I only come for the money!' Funnily enough we've never seen him since.

Dennis Jones worked for us for 25 years; he was our foreman and machine operator and worked days and nights. One morning I went in to find Dennis still on site and as white as a ghost. I asked him if he was OK. He said 'I've been chased round the steelworks by a huge bull, Al' He went on to explain that during his shift in the dark he'd been loading a trailer with his magnet and when he got out for a break he felt some hot air breathing on his neck. When he turned around he was eye to eye with this bull. He ran and the bull followed - he didn't stop running until he got to the lodge. It turned out that this bull had escaped from the local abattoir; it was dealt with by a police marksman.

I remember I once had reason to go to see Norman Green; I was after a little tipper for a job on the Steel Works and someone told me he had some BMCs for sale. So I went up to his office and there's old Norman, sitting in his chair with his pipe and his matches. I said 'Hello, I'm Alan Sturge, I understand you've got some trucks for sale.' 'Yes, I've got two Austins. Go have a look up the yard.' So I went up and thought one of them would do me fine. I went back to the office and asked him how much he wanted and he told me to make him an offer. I can remember I said 'I'll have one for £400.' He said 'Lad, come with me.' and he got out of his seat and we walked up the yard. He got the box of matches out of his pocket and said 'I'll set fire to it while you stand here.' I said, 'Well, you told me to make you an offer.' He said 'I'll not take less than £450.' I told him I was happy to give him the other £50 and bought it!

Other haulage firms on the steelworks in 1964 were Bassetts who had a lot of trailers in there and Critchlows, O Jones Transport, Don Smith, McVies from Scotland and Mountford Brothers. I remember Paul Dulson coming on when he was 21 and had just passed his test. He was driving an old Atki Borderer for Mountfords with a 40ft trailer on.

We did a lot of nights because at Christmas the steelworks' drivers wouldn't work so we had to cover. We also had to ferry the workers when the PMT went on strike in 1977. We rented five mini buses and ferried all three shifts. They were on strike for twelve weeks and shortly after that the Fire Brigade came out on strike so we had to cover for them as well. We had these little trucks with tanks on the back full of water. God knows what they would have put out if the steelworks had been on fire!

As the years went by we took on more responsibility. The steelworks was built to produce 6000 tons a week and the same plant, with a bit of tweaking here and there over the years, was producing 11,000 tons a week. This created a problem as some customers couldn't take their orders all at once so we were asked to become their on-site steel stockholder. We ended up with two 25 ton forklifts, two 25 ton cranes and a gang of men monitoring; we knew where all the stuff was and where it was going. In the late 1980s they got rid of the transport manager so I was asked if we would take the job, monitor the stuff and issue the work out to the other hauliers.

We didn't start moving the steel sections out until the 1980s. It was one bank holiday and

Saturday afternoon at the steel works. Vehicles loaded and ready to go out on Monday. Mid 1970s.
All photos Alan Sturge Collection

they'd got all these railway trucks loaded and the trains weren't operating. We were asked to give them a price to unload the trucks. We tried it one weekend and they asked us to do it on a regular basis because they were having a bit of trouble with the hauliers. So we bought a 25 ton mobile crane - and we did this job for about fifteen years. Then they asked us to put some flat trailers in to deliver steel. I bought a 60ft trombone and what I thought was a forty foot trailer but it was actually 50 ft and we operated it carrying long sections of steel.

With the uncertainty of the steel market it was apparent we needed to diversify so in 1996 we bought our first yard at Parkhouse Industrial Estate and formed Sturge (Bros) Trailers which was a company specialising in the manufacture and renovation of steel and alloy tipping trailers.

We finished at the steelworks when it closed in 2000 but continued doing general haulage from Parkhouse. We had 50 men at one time but it became such a headache that we decided to close down and sell everything. We all work for other people now; I have worked for Sainsbury's for 9 years and was due to retire last year but have decided to stay on for two days a week.

I started restoring vehicles about thirty years ago. A friend who is a school teacher used to come and work for me during the six week holiday and in his spare time he was doing an O type Bedford up. Anyway, I went and helped him and got the bug. I bought an S type Bedford from Watsons scrapyard at Stone and did that up and then I bought a little tipper that I've still got. I've restored eleven vehicles in the last thirty years and I've sold seven. My wife's quite happy to go along with it; some wives aren't. If you've got a wife who doesn't mind your hobbies then you're a very lucky man. She comes to all the shows with me.

I can drive for Sainsbury's in one of their trucks and get no pleasure out of it at all but when I get in one of the old ones and it's making lots of noise and shaking me all over the place, well, that's proper driving to me!

J L COOPER - Steven Cooper

My grandfather, John Lewis Cooper, was a farmer in Milton when he started the haulage business. He had three sons, Jack, Kenneth and my father, Stanley, as well as two daughters.

There were two sides to the business: haulage/warehousing and haulage/buying and selling of road building materials. The business operated from Church Garage in Milton running tippers carrying tarmac. In my granddad's day there was a tarmac plant just off the A53 near to where Aldi is now but it was moved down to the steel works in Shelton in the 1950s. We were operating out of Shelton Bar with tippers throughout this time and also had six vehicles doing the same work out of Shotton Steel Works. In about 1956 we built another depot in Foxley Lane, the first of two depots we had there. By this time we had branched out into warehousing and carrying goods for pottery firms and shipping agents. Goods were stored at the warehouse and taken to the docks on flats.

Once the business had moved it was decided to close Church Garage; there are houses there now. In 1961 we leased land behind the Foxley pub from the council and built more warehousing. At some stage during the move from Church Garage to Foxley we acquired another haulage firm, A W Lewis Hauliers.

I became involved in the business in about 1971 as a trainee transport manager. By this time we were leasing the ground floor of what was the Hardman Institute for offices. Roy Dutton was Transport Manager in those days alongside a shipping manager, John Mason. Brian Hardy took over this position when John sadly passed away. We also had an office manager, Harold Holdcroft. The business was quite big, probably about 50 vehicles then. Harry Kirkham was in charge of the warehouse and Dave Bough took over from Charlie Pegg as the garage foreman. Charlie had been with the company virtually from the beginning.

I remember one of our drivers, Terry Eardley, making all the national headlines when he turned a coal lorry over going round a bend with 15 tons of coal on. He smashed up against a doorway and on the door was a note 'Coalman, No coal today!'

During the early 1990s there was a steady decline in warehousing and haulage and we decided to sell the tractor units and trailers; we did a deal with John Fernyhough who took them all. Brian Hardy went to work for John and stayed there until his retirement. We continued to run what was J L Cooper and Sons from the original 1956 yard with a fleet of about nine tippers but later sold those to Dave Weaver. We sold the last of our lorries on New Year's Eve 1999 and became a property company.

A line-up of Cooper's vehicles in the yard.

An S type Bedford artic at the
Foxley Lane, Depot

When Derek Rhead started these O types were
being used on tarmac and quarry work at
Cauldon. Scammell couplings

Derek Rhead

I'd been riding in J L Cooper lorries since I was a lad because my uncles Lija and Jack worked there and sometimes took me out with them delivering tarmac. When I left school in 1959 I went to work for Coopers as well. At that time they were at the main garage at the side of Milton church and were in the process of building the depot in Foxley Lane. I moved almost straight away to the Foxley site and worked in the yard helping load the wagons. In those days there were no forklifts or anything like that; I drove an old Fordson tractor that had hooks on it for the pottery cages. We also transported pottery in barrels. The vehicles were all Bedfords.

We did a hell of a lot down at the Michelin; I'd have to go down with the drivers early in the morning to help them load tyres because it was all done by hand then. I passed my test at 17 in a little Bedford and started going round the Potteries bringing loads back to the depot. When I was 21 I automatically went on to artics because in those days you didn't have to apply for an artic licence. We used to do a lot of steel out of Shelton Bar that went all over the country. Mountford Brothers, Bassetts, Alcocks and Sturges were all on Shelton at the time.

I remember when I first went on my own I bought a BMC Mastiff bulk powder tanker which I'd driven for Coopers from new. I stayed with Coopers but operated on a subcontract basis.

This is taken at the Five Towns Tarmacadam site on Shelton steel works.
An S type petrol Bedford but would possibly be converted to diesel.

An 'O' type - could be Redland, Cauldon.

A Bedford Scammell OSS at Liverpool Docks.

BELOW
A Cooper vehicle at Liverpool Docks

The yard at Milton

'Mogger' Williams
with new No 9.

A Seddon Atki

Kevin Williams who
was part-time
mechanic and driver
with an Iveco.

Later I had a Volvo F86 and an F88. I was with them until they closed down. Through Coopers I'd been doing Canadian Pacific container work out of Tilbury (later at Felixstowe) so I continued loading and delivering containers all over the country. My son, Andrew came to work for me when he was 17 and when he was 21 we got a bigger artic so he was then running alongside me. We now have six artic units and three rigids and operate from Canal Street, Longport.

A Volvo that Derek Rhead bought from Moorlock to use on Coopers. *Derek Rhead*

Ted Selby

I worked for Coopers for 39 years. When I first went there I was driving a Bedford KM with a bulk powder tanker but later drove an ERF, a Leyland Marathon, a Leyland Road Train and an Iveco.

I remember one afternoon I was driving the Marathon through Abbey Hulton when I hit the bridge. A lump of stone fell and lodged itself between the trailer and tractor legs. I was trying to back up when the police arrived; they contacted the office and the garage blokes came out to tow the lorry back. When we got to the yard I was going to the washroom to wash my face when Steven Cooper saw me and told me to go to the hospital. I hadn't realised that my face was covered in blood; I'd got glass pieces in it from the windscreen. I think I was lucky I wasn't more seriously hurt. If I'd been driving an ERF with a solid steering column I would probably

Ted Selby in his Iveco with electric sheet.
Ted drove this for Coopers and also when he went to Weavers.
Taken in 1999 just before he retired. *Ted Selby*

have broken my legs but fortunately the Marathon's column gave way and let me go. My CB 'handle' was Marathon Man but after the incident with the bridge I became Bridge Bender.

On one occasion one of our drivers was driving through Nottingham when he spotted a Scania. Now Scanias were new and there were very few around at the time. Our driver hadn't seen one before and was so busy watching this vehicle that he went through the lights on red - the car in front stopped but he didn't! It was really funny because when the police asked him what had happened he started telling them that he was so busy looking at this 'fantastic' new wagon that he hadn't seen the lights change!

A BMC with a Laird cab (later called a boxer cab). Used
for multi-drops in the North East for Michelin tyres
going to Newcastle, Darlington and Bishop Auckland.

Ted leaning against the ERF he drove for quite a while
after he had come off artics. c1994. *Ted Selby*

A line up in the yard.
All Photos unless otherwise stated Cooper Collection

NORMAN GREEN - Philip Green

My grandfather, Norman Green started his business in Warrington Street, Fenton originally with horses and carts. I can remember the old fitter, Mol Hulme talking about Grandfather buying a couple of old lorries and he and Mol made one vehicle out of the two. This was his first lorry. At some stage he moved to Atlas Street from where the business really took off.

Dad had three brothers who worked in the business: Eric ran the garage; Frank ran the coal yard and Billy drove a six wheeler. When Frank passed away Billy took over his job in the coal yard. My father, Norman Jr ran the coal side.

Grandfather bought another depot in Portland Road, Longton, from where he ran the haulage side. I left school and didn't know what I wanted to do so I joined the business working in the garage. At first I was sweeping up, making tea and helping out but I eventually got my HGV and went on to another side of the business called Potteries Fuel Supplies, driving tankers.

Norman Green with his first vehicle, a Morris Commercial. The girl could be one of his sisters.

Grandfather ran about 100, a mixture of flat beds, tippers, artics etc. He took over a number of local companies; I remember he took on the haulage side of Maiden and Ellis from Wolstanton and also a company called Dilhorne Coal as well as Baddeley Green Haulage. He had a couple of vans delivering school meals. He also had a fleet of five or six small white lorries working for Hargreaves Mill in Fenton carrying clay mixtures etc in tubs and sacks. There was another mill opposite the top of Duke Street; I can't remember what it was called but the drivers left their vehicles there at night. We only saw these lorries when they were broken down or needed servicing.

There was also a paraffin delivery operation. Then of course, he had his coal lorries. Most of the flats that carried bags of coal were eventually taken on by the drivers and operated on an owner/driver basis. He had about 70 tippers, mostly Albions and Dodges, running with bulk coal to places like BICC near Chester, Bengers Food Factory (Fisons) in Holmes Chapel, Meaford Power Station, Earls Cement at Waterhouses and ICI at Runcorn. We had two or three that used to go to Parkhouse Brickworks, where Fedex is now, taking coal. I remember we had a couple of flats running out of there too, carrying bricks. Obviously, we used to pick up coal from the collieries and deliver to coal merchants. Merchants who didn't have their own tippers would ring Granddad up and say 'I'm allocated 10 tons from Florence can you sort it out for me?' We had some smaller lorries going into the gasworks picking coke up and delivering to schools in Newcastle and Stoke.

Jack Davis, the accountant, left with Norman Jr on the right.

Norman standing outside the garage.

Taken at Atlas Street. L-R: Frank Lynch, ?, Eric Green, Jack Davis, ? .

The vehicle is probably a 4D Ford

BELOW
The site at Meir Hay Wharf

We don't know who the men are but the vehicle is probably a Morris Commercial.

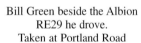

Bill Green beside the Albion RE29 he drove.
Taken at Portland Road

A Dodge Kew with the later grill.

A Seddon at Meir
Haye Wharf

A new ERF KV
bought for the brick
job at Holditch

BELOW
The same vehicle
loaded with bricks
from Holditch.

Norman taken at Meir Hay Wharf

As the company grew we needed more space so Grandfather bought the depot in Kendrick Street, Longton. He sold the Atlas Street and Portland Road depots so the entire business could operate from the one site; this would be about 1966. He had about twelve acres in total at Kendrick Street, about eight acres of tarmac and a massive garage.

In the 1970s there was the miners' strike which we coped with relatively well. I remember I had to go to the Union HQ in Stafford most days to get permission to go and pick up coal to take to hospitals. Unfortunately, after the miners had gone back our own drivers decided to strike but Grandfather felt the business couldn't stand paying higher wages so he decided to close down. He parked the vehicles up and I remember he asked me to go and get the tax discs out of the windows so he could surrender the tax on them. When people found out he was selling-up they came to buy the vehicles from him; some would buy just one and others would take two, three or four at a time. The Kendrick Street site is now a housing estate.

He sold Potteries Fuel Supplies, the company I worked for, to British Fuel Company and sold his coal business to National Fuel Distributors. I continued to work for British Fuel

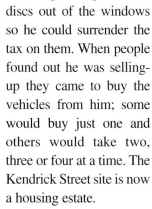

L-R: Philip Green, John ? , Harry Mountford, Kathleen Bradbury and Stewart Goddard.

Company who based themselves at the old Wolstanton Colliery. Later CPL took over both British Fuel Company and NFD and I continued to work for them for many years. I'm retired now and have no connection with haulage but my eldest son, Jamie is Operations Manager for Beresfords in London so he is continuing the family tradition in haulage.

L-R: Dick Morgan, Philip Green and Percy Foskitt.

John Collier MBE

My dad, Len Collier, worked for Norman driving a Bedford S type that Dave Hewson had been driving from new. I remember Norman swapped this Bedford for an old Foden and it was very low geared. It would go anywhere; my dad used to go to Whitehaven in it from Hilton Gravel and it used to take him two and a half days - this old Foden going along doing 25 mph, 30mph flat-out!

When I went to work for Norman in 1960 I went straight on to the Ford Trader that Clarence Willmore had from new. These Fords were OK but they had hopeless brakes on them. When I was at Plants they always fitted Hyrdrovaks on them. Anyway, the first day I drove this Ford I nearly went through a hedge at Wetley Rocks so when I got back I told Norman it was no use. He said 'What's up with it? Clarence has driven it.' I said 'I don't care what he's done; that wants a Hydrovak on.' 'Oh, yeah, Clarence has mentioned something about that. Take it to Salmon and Jones's tomorrow and get one fitted.' So I did and after that it was like driving a Rolls Royce.

I worked for him for about eight years and he was a brilliant man to work for; straight as a die. He knew all his drivers and took an interest in them. I remember I was renting a two-up, two-down house when the kids were young and it was damp and cold. When I told Norman he said 'I tell you what, you go and buy yourself a house, not a big one and I'll stand as guarantor.' That's the man he was. I said 'Howd on, what if I dunner want to work for you anymore?' He said 'No problem. I don't want you to leave me, you're a good worker, but I shonner fall out with you if you want to leave.'

I remember we had a bloke named Freddie Lloyd, a little stout bloke, who used to draw alongside a coal lorry with his Dodge Kew highsider and he'd scramble up and chuck two load out of a coal wagon with a shovel. He was a strong man. Then there was Arthur Hubbard from Caverswall who used to go up to Norman's pig farm at Meir Heath to help out. Len Smallwood, Edward Dawson, Roy Beech and a bloke named Ray Davies who used to do a bit of singing in the clubs were all there the same time as me. Then there was Howard Massey, Tommy Rushton and Joe Ferber. I remember there was a bloke we used to call 'Little Eric' (Mason), always wore a tam, who'd been with Norman for years; he was one of the best.

I was working on contract down at Hilton Gravel and Norman used to say, 'The only time I want to see you, John is when you come for your money or to fill up. I don't want to see you any other time.' I used to go in on a Tuesday at about 8.00 at night to take my time sheet in. I'd go in the portacabin and Norman would be there behind this big desk with all these pieces of paper with lorry numbers on spread over it - he had about 100 vehicles at this time - surveying these papers just like a general planning a battle. He'd go and get my money and he'd say 'Everything alright, Mister? Keep an eye on them tyres.' That would be it and off I'd go.

I left because I'd had enough of driving - going out on cold, foggy days with no heaters or anything. I heard there was a job going at Hilton Gravel on the quarry and decided to go there. The last time I saw Norman he was filling his car up at Times Service Station down the Tean Road after he'd finished with lorries and we stood talking for ages.

909 MEH, the Ford Trader Clarence Willmore had driven before John. *Photo John Collier*

This Albion could have been made into a six wheeler later. Dougie Wild of Vauxhall Street, Longton always painted Norman's vehicles.

Roy Goldstraw who worked in the office with Norman. c1960

Seddon. We have no information on this one, perhaps someone reading this will remember it.

John Willmore

I went to work for Norman Green in 1965 working in the garage. My dad, Clarence (sometimes known as Jim) had driven Norman's Foden MVT 610. My dad left and went back again (a lot of drivers did this in those days) and when he returned he had the new Ford Trader, 909 MEH.

My first job every day was to sweep the garage because everything had to be kept immaculate. I remember when they moved to Meir Haye Wharf (Kendrick Street) the garage floor was painted and had under-floor heating. Every morning we had to do the tyres; I would be working with Mick Moody and we'd have to rub the inner tubes with this wire scrubbing tool and put vulcanised patches on. I remember one time the scrubbing tool went missing and Mick said 'Don't worry, John it'll come back.' and, sure enough, it did - inside one of the tyres!

My other duty was driving the loading shovel. Norman had a contract taking road salt down south and it was my job to load the vehicles. This went on for a while until they noticed that the salt had started to rot the bodies so they had to change from aluminium to wooden or steel bodied lorries. I'd also go to major pot banks with this shovel loading 'seconds' that were taken to Longton Hall tip. Hundreds of tons of what looked like perfect ware were dumped there! I've often wondered if people went on there to get this stuff because it seemed such a waste.

They had a Leyland 20 van that I used to pick spares up in or go out to breakdowns. I wanted to go on the lorries but Norman wanted me in the garage. I remember once they were stuck for a driver and asked me to take a coal wagon to deliver coke to Madeley Primary School. I'd be about seventeen and I remember it was a boiling hot day. When I got there I had to carry these sacks quite a long way and up a lot of steps. I was really hot and all I could think of was getting down to the shop to get a drink. Anyway, when I finished I dashed off and got a drink and when I set off back I saw all these coal bags strewn over the road. I remember wondering who might have dropped them (they were very expensive to buy) until I realised it was me. In my haste to get away I'd forgotten to put the weight on the bags and they'd blown off.

Norman was a good man to work for; you were always treated with great respect. My father wouldn't have a word said against him. Your wages were always right - if you worked fifty hours you were paid for fifty hours. He was very straight.

Norman was in charge and his son, Norman Jr worked there too. Norman's brother Eric was Garage Manager and his other brother, Bill drove a Dodge. Mol Hulme did the engines, Roy Benton was Foreman, Gordon Wilson was on the bodies and Richard Howell was welding.

I left Norman in 1968 and went to work for Dave Weaver who allowed me to drive full-time. I really enjoyed the job picking milk up from farms and also helping around the farm after daily duties. Looking back it was a most enjoyable job; the farmers looked forward to you coming down the lane and some would have a cup of tea waiting.

After Weavers I went to Hulland Gravel but I spent my last working years at JCB. When I retired my wife bought me a retirement present - a Bedford O Series. I'd tried to buy this same vehicle the year before in Scotland but had just missed it. I discovered completely by chance that its new home was in Denstone. Anyway, the owner, Alan Ratcliffe was prepared to sell so she went ahead and bought it for me. It's given me a great deal of pleasure restoring it.

I have recently written a book *My love of Life, Lorries and Coaches* which covers my life up to when I was fifteen and am now planning to write Part 2.

John Willmore with his restored Bedford O Series at Froghall Wharf. *John Willmore.*

Frank Lynch is first left on the lorry with Norman's brother Ernie on the right. We don't have names for the other men or the two office girls.

BELOW
Norman Jr with his Citroen on a day out with his family c1960s

The offices at Meir Hay Wharf with Norman Jr's Zodiac parked in front.

Bill Hazleton started working for PFS in 1981. The shows him with his vehicle and his son, Robert, on a dinner break outside his home.
Bill Hazleton

Bill Hazleton in 1971 when he was 21 and working in the garage at Meir Hay Wharf. Bill started when John Willmore left.
Bill Hazleton

TERRY LEWIS

I started in transport when I was 21 in 1964 working for Berresfords at Cheddleton. Their main thing was buses, obviously but they had lorries as well - Thames Traders and other things. Every day was an adventure on there. We delivered sand bags to all the pits around the country and did work for Tempo Beams; we'd deliver these beams to all the building sites.

I loaded out of Burslem one day with an old Thames Trader and it was knocking so I called back at the garage and there was Johnny Morris, the mechanic. He went upstairs and got a set of big ends and Jimmy (Berresford) wrote down on a piece of paper all the spanner sizes I needed and we got under the wagon. He showed me that if you undid the nuts up on the front axle you could prop your feet on the front axle and hold the sump up while you undid the rest. Then you could lower it down and put it up without changing the oil and he showed me this sealant stuff that had recently been brought out. Anyway, I came along by Sheffield Wednesday football ground this day and it just went bang. Across the road was a garage so I went over and asked the bloke if he could lend me these spanners that I had listed. He looked at me and I said 'and have you got this gasket seal stuff? He says 'What are you going to do?' I said 'That wagon over there, the big end's gone on it. I'm going to change it.' He says 'What about the oil?' I said 'Oh, no I don't need oil.' He kept looking at me like I'd gone out! 'Well, you cheeky young bastard, I'll lend you the bloody spanners if you're willing to do that.' So I dropped the sump off, got this gasket seal and put these second-hand shells in. I got in the cab and started up and they were worse than what I'd taken out! In the end I stayed the night at a nearby pub and Mick Birley picked me up and we towed it back.

I was broken down one day and was in the garage when someone said the two-o-clock from Hanley's got a broken spring. Well, this particular bus was the Hanley to Leek and they used to change over conductor and driver at the garage. It was an ex-Stockport Corporation double decker. Jimmy tells me to go up to the stores and get a spring for when it gets in. So along it comes with this spring gone and the driver drives it in over the pit and we changed the spring and never took the passengers off. Well, we'd got nowhere to put them!

A lot of drivers came and went. On Jimmy's it was five shillings an hour and as many as you could do and this lad who'd driven for him for years kept saying 'I'll take me wages home in a wheelbarrow one day.' It must have got to Jimmy so one Friday he says, 'Go fetch a wheelbarrow.' This lad says 'What?' Jimmy says, 'Well, you want to take your wages home in a wheelbarrow so you can this week.' He got all his wages in pennies and halfpennies in this wheelbarrow!

Jimmy Berresford would never leave people stranded - whatever the weather his buses always turned out - hail, rain or snow. He was also a brilliant engineer; he lifted the garage piece by piece, section by section so it could take double-deckers. He cut the stanchions through and jacked them up so far and welded them.

When I worked for Comart I was going abroad with beef from Ireland. They bought three Hinos with Irish registrations; they were evil motors. I went to Portugal in one - you could be driving down the road and pull the gear stick out of its socket and just bob it back in again. The bed in it was a bit like the Bedford TK really, it was a shelf in the back but the windows sloped in on you. The heater was a hole the size of an old half-crown for the heat to come out.

My first trip was beef to Paris. I decided to take my dad with me and we'd got to go to this big new market just outside Paris but when we arrived there was a change and we had to take the load to a cold storage depot. So they gave me this address and it was back to Paris by the Seine at about

6.00am. Anyway, I'm asking different people where it was and I'm pointing to the map. Just now I see this bloke coming up in a suit and carrying a brief case and I'm thinking he's educated; he'll speak English. So I ask him. He says to me 'You are English?' I told him I was and he says, 'I speak perfect English; I don't understand you.' My dad puts his head through the window and says, 'Dust ere, ar youth, thay'st pulled up, jumped ite an' nearly knocked 'im dine and then thee says 'Cost tell us weir this is, youth?' This man hadn't got a clue what we were saying. I'll never forget his face, he was totally bewildered.

I worked for Comart a couple of times as well as Moorlock and Beresfords of Tunstall. I used to meet

On the French side of Mont Blanc.

up with Alfie Booth, Ted Morgan, Dave Scarlett and Stan Jukes when we were on our travels. After Beresfords I had my own vehicle for a time and then I went for Shirley's.

LEFT
Waiting on the dock in Tripoli. Drivers had to re-register lorries to Libyan plates. This would be a return as the foreign plates are still on. You had to catch the same ferry you arrived in so you could get your plates back - this could take up to three weeks. Obviously, a booze-free zone, so real fun!

On the Kodak run, Lisbon. Mid 1970s. Wife Beryl in cab with children, Matt and Becky. All photos Terry Lewis

On the docks at Patras, Greece. Once, Terry and 15 other drivers from various countries were held there for 51 days as the French beef they'd brought wasn't acceptable. They had to freeze it and eventually were forced to take it back. When they got to Ancona they were held there for four days before finally being taken by police escort to Mont Blanc.

RAY GOULD

My first driving job was for Norman Green on tippers when I was 21. I think I was on a Leyland Comet taking coal from the collieries, Hem Heath mostly, to places like Meaford Power Station and RAF Cosford. I was there for quite a while but because I was living at Porthill I decided to go to a guy named Bloor who had three Thames Traders at Vale View in Porthill. After that I did a stint at Downings Bricks driving a Foden eight wheeler and then a year on the buses for PMT before going to Mountfords on steel.

It was interesting at Mountfords because they were doing these long wide loads and police escort loads. It was all coming out of Shelton Bar and it was good stuff. I remember when they were doing the Anchor Project at Scunthorpe the steel erectors always wanted the steel from Shelton because the measurements were always right; Shelton was the best in the country. When the erectors saw us coming they'd say 'We'll do this' because they knew they could get their bonus by putting it together quickly.

Louis DeCecco, one of the four people who started Comart, with the first Comart vehicle, a Scania left-hooker.

I first drove abroad when I went to work for Comart. My first journey was to Luxemburg and I went out with Alf 'Wheeler' Williams. Wheeler was a nice lad who had a very bad accident in Germany. It wasn't his fault, he swung to miss someone and went over a bridge and on to a motorway below. The air ambulance came and took him to hospital. I went to see him at Sneyd Green and thought he would never get over it but he did and he went back driving.

I didn't stay long at Comart because I got a job at Thor where Alan Dale was Transport Manager. He was a great bloke. If you did your job he was sound. I remember we were in the yard one day and there was a driver who didn't want to go on a journey. He said to me 'You take this load, Ray.' Anyway, Alan comes up and says 'What's up?' So this guy says 'I can't go, Alan, I've spent all day in the yard; I've dirtied my jeans, and everything.' Alan says 'Go down to Longton and get yourself a new pair of jeans and whatever you need and bring the bill back, no cost to you. You can still go.' Then he found another excuse and Alan sorted that as well. In the end he put this bloke in the position where he'd got to say he was finishing or go on the trip. He went on the trip.

We had some great times working on Thor; we were all really close. I did Baghdad two or three times, they really liked us out there. When you got to Ankara it was all dirt roads and no road signs - you'd get to this particular spot where you went right for Iraq and left for Iran. Later on they put road signs up!

If you broke down when you were abroad in those days there would be a line of wagons there to help. I remember going through the border into Tehran one day and I pulled on to this big café car park. There was a Frenchman there with a Volvo and he was stuck. Anyway, this Hungarian sent him over and said 'Go ask Thor' because we got on really well with the Hungarians; they always had lots of spares and would always let you have them at no cost. Anyway, I went in my box and got the hose out that he needed and he said 'How much?' I said 'No, no you give it to me next time I see you.' I looked up and the Hungarians were watching me and they put their thumbs up. That's what it was like because you wouldn't see anyone stuck.

I remember there was a lad we used to see from time to time when we went out there; I can't remember who he drove for. He had an accident when he was driving though this town when a child ran out of a bus queue straight into the side of the wagon. Of course he pulled up and this

Duncan Gould in front of Ray's Thor motor.

Alan Dale, a subbie for Chapman and Ball, taking time out.
Alan was a popular driver who went out to the Middle East in an ERF 5MW, HRF 583N, during the 1970s. Alan told his son, Alan Jr, of an occasion when he had a problem with his engine and Ian Tyler towed him up every hill from Tehran to Jugoslavia. Alan passed away in 2006. If anyone has a picture of his ERF please get in touch as Alan Jr would be very interested. *Alan Dale Jr*

child was in a bad way but the people started stoning him so he got back in the wagon and drove to the nearest police station. He told them what had happened and they took his particulars and told him he could go. Just as he was going this car pulled up with these people in and they'd got the child with them; they hadn't gone to the hospital. Anyway, the police had a change of heart and took him to prison. I'd gone through this town and didn't know anything had happened but when I got to Tehran some blokes I knew said he was locked up. He was in there for ages and when he went to court the judge just said '20 years'. When he tried to explain they told him to write out what had happened, which he did. Well, that wouldn't do because they said it had to be in Farsi which, of course, he couldn't do. Then they told him to draw a sketch of how it happened and the judge said 'Oh, ten years, then.' He was put in a cell with about twelve other people and it was terrible, just a dirt floor and no toilets. Some of the lads used to go to see him when they were going through and give him what they could. He did a few months, I think. I can remember seeing him after he came out and he said that he'd never go again. He was a really nice bloke.

One of the blokes I'd see when I was out there was Alan Dale. Alan was a subbie for Chapman and Ball and drove an ERF. We were in my vehicle one day going in to town to make a phone call and this driver cut us up really badly. Alan jumped out and grabbed hold of him and slammed him on to the bonnet a couple of times because it could have caused a serious accident. I got out and could see about six policemen across the road and was trying to tell him. Anyway, they came across and I thought we were in for it but they told us to get on our way because they'd seen what had happened and took this bloke off.

After Thor I went to Pandoro but it was too regimental. Anyway, because I knew Dennis Moore and Maurice Locket from my time on Comart and they were running Moorlock, I went to them. It was funny because I went for the job and they set me on but when I came out of the office I saw a mate of mine - 'The Monk' - and he said, 'How many drivers do they want, Ray?' I told him that it was just one and I'd been given the job. Anyway, as I was already in work and he wasn't I went back in and asked them if they'd give him the job and give me a ring when the next vacancy came up. So that's what they did and after about five weeks Dennis rang and said

'Ray, that job's going, do you want it?'

I enjoyed working for them; it was fridges going all over Europe. Eddie DeVille, Johnny Bradburn (The Monk) and Ron Bates were there the same time as me. Then Ian Adams came and Alan Rigby, Albert Rushton and Frankie Breeze.

When Moorlock finished I went to Tideswells and ended up at Shirley's. I retired 2 years ago.

Ray in Madrid in DEH 800W. The one alongside, XFA 484S was Ray's old vehicle but driven here by Cliff Rowley.

Ray coming out of a village in Spain. All photos unless otherwise stated Ray Gould

WINFIELD TRANSPORT GROUP Warren Winfield

My grandfather, Harry Winfield set up the business in about 1954 moving coal and coke to power stations, factories and schools. The business was based at Wolverhampton Street, Walsall then. Up until 1968 grandfather ran 12 vehicles but was actually running a fleet of 100 subcontract lorries.

In 1969 when the coal job died grandfather didn't want to be involved in transport anymore and decided to concentrate on his other business interests - the Kingfisher Country Club at Kingswinsford and the Parlour's Hall Hotel in Bridgnorth. Meanwhile my dad, Sid, made the decision to go into contract hire while his brother John ran a skip hire business from a depot in Shortacre Street, Walsall. The contract hire, based by this time at Norton Canes, continued into the mid-1980s when the job changed again and we became general hauliers. When father died in 1983 I took over the business with my mother, Jenni; we ran it together until she retired in 2001. We are now based in Hawks Green, Cannock and I run the company with my wife, Alison and sister, Karen.

Vince Cooke

I went to work for Harry Winfield in 1957 and stayed there for about five years. There were some real characters there; I remember Georgie Brown who was a tall, strong guy and George Healey. I was driving a Comet ODH 714 at first, which was the first Leyland Comet they had. George Healey had it before me. Then I had WBH 651, bringing coal from Kingsbury and North Warwick Collieries into Birmingham. I also did nights to South Wales bringing coke back to the Midlands.

A Saturday morning job would be fetching vehicles from Measham Auctions because Harry used to buy and sell vehicles alongside the haulage. I remember one Saturday morning Harry took me and Georgie Brown to fetch two wagons he'd bought and we went in his Rolls Royce. Anyway, he called in to see someone in Birmingham and we were waiting for quite a long time in the car and were getting hungry so we got some fish and chips. When he came out of his meeting and saw us eating fish and chips in his Rolls he wasn't best pleased!

I also remember him standing in the yard one morning when one of the drivers walked past wearing drainpipe trousers, low shoes and white socks. He said 'Who's that?' Someone said 'He's a driver' 'Not here he's not! This is a transport yard not a dance hall.' So he sacked him. He set him on again in the afternoon, though.

During my holidays when I was working for S Jones I would do a bit for Sid, driving an FG Austin doing multi-drop deliveries around Coventry and Birmingham.

This line up of mainly Comets with an old Hippo. The house at the end was the offices with a flat upstairs that 'Fred' the yardman lived in. Vince remembers the Hippo very well: *'When you got to a roundabout in the Hippo it was easier to keep right than left!' Winfield Collection*

ABOVE
Winfields operated 112
vehicle fleet transporting
coal from local pits to
power stations, schools
and factories.
The first vehicle on the
right, just visible, is 650
FDH, Leyland Comet
that Vince had from new.
1958.
Winfield Collection

ABOVE & LEFT
Vince Cooke standing beside the Leyland Steer he
drove which was ex-Samuel Tandy - waiting to be
painted so still in Tandy colours.
Vince Cooke Collection

S. JONES - Michael Jones

My grandfather, Samuel 'Sammy' Jones became a haulage contractor in Aldridge in 1914 transporting his first consignment, reputedly cases of crockery, from Aldridge railway station by horse and cart to the local Manor House. By 1920 he had acquired his first motor lorry, a Thorneycroft and a few years later was employing Bill Cooper Sr to drive a second vehicle. 'Dad' Cooper stayed with the company for many years until his retirement.

Sammy Jones, the founder of the company, with his Thorneycroft.
Jones Collection

My father, Samuel Edward Jones, took over the business in 1936. Over the next 25 years he built up a large fleet of tipper lorries operating from a yard in Walsall Wood Road, Aldridge. We lived in a bungalow that backed on to the yard so I grew up seeing all the lorries coming and going and I remember as a youngster sitting on the bonnet of a vehicle driven by Tommy Sedgwick. One of my earliest memories was listening to Frank Hicken, my father's right hand man, in the traffic office telling Tommy off for something he'd done; it was frightening. My father and Frank made a fantastic partnership; Father was the businessman and Frank was the man who made it all happen. All the drivers loved Frank and would do anything for him even though he cursed and swore at them.

In the mid-1950s the local council decided they didn't want all our trucks, sixty to seventy by this time, queuing up Walsall Wood Road every night waiting to fuel-up so we moved to our present location in Anglian Road which was the old cement works.

I joined the company in 1962 working under Frank and learning the business. Under my father's leadership the business grew and in the mid 1970s we became ERF Main Distributors because at the time ERFs were very much in demand and we were finding it difficult to get hold of them. We secured the dealership on condition we employed Reg Johnson as Sales Manager and I remember he'd get very frustrated when we'd take the trucks he wanted to sell for the haulage side. At one time we were running over 100 ERFs and Leylands.

We certainly employed some 'talented' people over the years, none more so than the driver who took a load of slack to Dickinsons at Watford but instead of delivering it he brought it back and donated it to his neighbours. He'd managed to get his note signed but had actually tipped the load in the street; people were out with their shovels and wheelbarrows helping themselves. When we found out we had to go to see the customer to explain and, of course, we had to pay!

At some stage my father bought Chambers of Stafford who had a contract with Dunlop carrying tyres and this was the start of the general haulage side of the business. It was clear that the business was expanding rapidly and we needed someone to run the general haulage. Frank Hicken was still the senior man but Bill Cooper came into the office to take care of the general side. Bill (Dad Cooper's son) had been working for us as a driver but now became a hugely important influence in what was a growing aspect of the business.

Then containerization came along. We were approached by Duramin who wanted us to store the containers they were building for Dartline. Over the years we'd added more land to the original site and were ideally placed to accommodate them. This side of the business grew and we became one of the largest shipping container depots in the Midlands storing, repairing and maintaining many thousands of containers every year. For a time we also operated a freight forwarding and consolidation business and set up what became a major international ADR road tanker fleet transporting hazardous bulk liquids throughout Europe. We also set up the first HGV Driver Training School in the UK.

In 1976 we opened a container depot and transport company in Jeddah, Saudi Arabia. This came about when we employed an ambitious young guy in the traffic office named Dick Green. We were already doing some work on the Continent with tilts when he sent three trucks out to Doha in Qatar carrying electrical switch gear in tilt trailers. Unfortunately, one of these broke down at the top end of Saudi Arabia and was stranded over the Christmas holiday. It wasn't a good start but in spite of this we could see the potential in Saudi and decided to look into the possibility of working out there. Our accountants at the time had an office in Jeddah and introduced us to Abdullah and Said Binzagr who were the major importers in Saudi Arabia for many companies including Unilever and BAT. At the time they were finding it difficult to move the goods inside the kingdom so we came along at just the right time. We agreed terms and formed a partnership whereby we provided the trucks, drivers and expertise and they provided the working capital - we called the company Trans Arabia.

We sent out 10 trucks with drivers and support staff under the management of Ken Broster. It was quite an adventure at the time. As well as transporting container after container of cigarettes and shampoo etc we had to deal with some unusual events. When we first went over there were no proper roads so we needed double-drive trucks to go through the desert and I remember an occasion when our vehicles had to negotiate through massive boulders in river beds in order to deliver equipment to a copper mine. Our blokes over there earned good money and had lots of leave but not everyone could hack it and some came back. During the Gulf War there were certain times of day when our drivers weren't able to enter Riyadh because Iraq was firing scud missiles; they had to park up a few miles outside the city until it was clear.

Eventually, the tax breaks we'd enjoyed disappeared and it was no longer viable to continue so we sold out in 1998 after 22 years.

As we approach our 100th year of trading, the 'Sammy Jones' family business still operates from Anglian Road and, although we no longer run vehicles, our container business continues to grow and flourish. We are now one of the country's leading retailers and hirers of shipping containers; we have a container conversion business as well as a self-storage arm. My son, Andrew is now MD and runs the business together with Jill Buckland and our team of great managers but I hope I still have something to offer in my 70th year.

Over the years we've employed some clever men but without doubt the undisputed heroes were Frank Hicken, Bill Cooper and, of course, my dad.

An Albion Caledonian. The driver is Harold Barlow who came along with the vehicle when S Jones bought out Barlow and Sons of Bloxwich. No heaters in these so Harold used to drive with a candle on the dash to thaw the ice on the windscreen. 1960. *M Jones Collection*

A Morris Leader.
M Jones Collection

Are you on here? An S Jones gathering in 1971. The drivers receiving gold watches for 25 years' service from Edward Jones are:
L-R: Harold 'Cocker' Dollaway, Edward Jones presenting, Mackie Clarke, Harold Moore and Ray Tams. Sylvia Hall is standing behind Mrs Dorothy Jones on the right of the picture. Others identified are: Iris Evans, Christine Jones (Michael's sister), Edith Jukes, Tony Waldron, Bill Cooper, Sid Bishop, Frank Hicken, Fred Forrester, Cliff Stringer, Bill Cooper Sr.
M Jones Collection.

LEFT
Still friends, L-R: Bill Cooper, Frank Hicken and Michael Jones. Taken in Michael's office 2012.
Michael Jones.

Frank Hicken

Before I left school I had a Saturday job at Aston's Bakery in Aldridge delivering bread but my first proper job, when I was fourteen, was working in the office at Electrical Conduits. By the time I left I was running the stores and going to their other depots checking the stock etc.

During this time I'd joined the Territorial Army so I was among the first to be sworn in to go to war in 1939; I wasn't quite eighteen. For the first twelve months I was a driving instructor at Whittington Barracks in Lichfield before volunteering with my best mate, Dougie Whitehouse to train as a blacksmith - that's how stupid it was at the time! Then we volunteered as carrier drivers in the Middle East but we

Lance Corporal Hicken aged 18. *Frank Hicken*

never actually got there; we ended up in Kano in Nigeria training young Nigerians. We formed what was the 81st West African Frontier Force. Eventually I went up in Burma where, on the first day of action, Dougie was killed - we were just a few yards apart. When 1945 came round I was sent to Germany in charge of guarding German POWs in hospitals. I came back to England in April 1946, having done six and a half years.

When I came home I got married and I remember I had £98 in my account from the army so I needed to find a job quickly. My sister knew Nadine Jukes who worked in the office at S Jones and asked her if Mr Jones wanted drivers. Fortunately, he said yes and set me on. For the first couple of weeks I was mating Sam Kimberley, shovelling coal but one day we were coming out of Rugeley and saw another of Jones's wagons coming the other way with a young lad driving it. That young lad was Billy Cooper; he was 16, no licence, and had brought an empty wagon out to me because a driver hadn't turned up and there were loads to be done. From then on I was driving.

One night, a couple of years later, Edward (Jones) was complaining about all the jobs he'd got to do and I said 'I could do it on my head.' and his reply was 'Well, you'd better come in and bloody

Frank Hicken in a Morris Saurer he drove for a while. This was what they called the junior version - the revs were governed so there was no speeding. This was one of two brand new ones S Jones bought. Note the 'suicide' doors. *M Jones collection.*

do it, then!' so I that's how I started my office life with S Jones. It was just the three of us doing the office work at that time: Edward, me and Lilian Dando who had taken over when Nadine passed away. Edward was a nice man and we worked well together. I used to sit in the garage with the books doing the adding up and multiplying in my head. Gradually the company grew and I became Transport Manager. At this time it was all coal on flats with sides on so the men were shovelling on, shovelling off, seven or eight tons a time, five loads a day.

As the business grew we got into tippers with drop-sides so we could take coal to the brickworks and return with bricks. In the 1960s we had Bill Cooper in the office because we were expanding so fast it became impossible to do everything. I thought if he was as good in the office as he was at his driving then he'd be excellent and he was. He didn't swear when he started but I taught him!

A guy named Billy Smith wanted us to buy his business; he ran four, four-wheel gravel tippers and, against our better judgement, we bought the company. He came to work for us with four drivers. It didn't make sense really because it was only long-distance tipper work that made money but we got four good drivers out of it: Pete Ellis, Mick Ellis, Graham Gooch and Ernie Stringer.

I finished up Transport Director and in 1986 was going to retire but Michael asked me to stay on part-time to look after the tachos etc. I did it for 5 years and left in 1991 after 45 years.

Gordon Taylor

My dad, Bill, worked for S Jones when Sammy Jones was running it. Everybody knew my dad as Big Bill. One Saturday morning he was going down to London Brick at Calvert, Bucks in a new Thorneycroft. It was a very windy day and he was driving down this road in Aynho when a tree blew over and crashed down on his cab. He was in convoy with 3 or 4 other Jones vehicles at the time so the other drivers were there to help him. His hands were trapped on the steering wheel but they managed to free him and get him to hospital.

Big Bill Taylor's Thorneycroft Amazon six wheel bulk tipper converted from an ex MOD Coles Crane. S Jones had two of these; Dad Cooper drove the other one. *Gordon Taylor*

Abe Anslow (left) with Big Bill in front of AEC 8 wheel bulk tipper which was ex Bowater Paper Mills. *Gordon Taylor*

Gordon standing in front of the Thorneycroft Amazon his dad drove. c 1950. Gordon Taylor

I also went to work for S Jones; I was a trailer mate to Ernie Smith when I was 16 and when I was old enough I became a driver. I remember driving an old Maudslay once with Bill Cooper sitting in the passenger seat. So there's Bill engrossed in *The Sporting Life* and I'm driving down Dumblederry Lane. I don't know what happened but I just touched the kerb and we ended up in the ditch. He only laughed; in fact he always talks about it whenever I see him.

Bill Cooper

My dad, Bill Sr, was the first driver Sammy Jones employed. At that time, about 1928, Sam only had two vehicles so he drove one and my dad the other.

I used to go with my father in his lorry from a young age. During the war fuel was difficult to get hold of so my dad's vehicle had two big cylinders at the back of the cab. One of these cylinders had a fire in that created coke fumes and these fumes went to the other cylinder and powered the vehicle. I remember one night during the war the Germans dropped a bomb down by the Chester Road, probably three quarters of a mile away from the depot. Anyway, a group of us were in the garage and heard it whistle before it landed so we knew it was going to be close. Nobody said a word as we all dived under this motor but I picked the side where the fire was, didn't I!

I started working for S Jones officially in 1944 when I was fourteen and did various jobs either in the garage or mating. When I was seventeen I started driving. I remember the company bought two new Morris Commercials Frank Hicken had one and I had the other. At that time Frank's mate was Ray Tams and mine was Rocky Derry who was a real tough guy.

When I was eighteen I went into the army to do my National Service, serving with the South Staffords in Hong Kong. When I came out and went back to S Jones, Frank had been promoted to the office. I went back on driving and I did my first trip to London. I was driving a vehicle with a cracked block and had to keep stopping and finding a ditch so I could fill a can with water to top it up. These were the things we had to do in the early years - we never thought anything of it.

I remember in the 1950s we had Leyland Comet four wheelers. The Comet was the best and most advanced vehicle at the time with an Eaton two-speed axle that you could drive like a car. After you'd been driving them for a while and you were really good, you could change down a full gear and at the same time change up half a gear you'd go down the full gear on the gear box but up half a gear on the button.

We used to have tippers taking coal down to all the different London brickworks and to Dickinson's Paper Mills at Watford and Hemel Hempstead. After the war a lot of buildings were being knocked down so we brought scrap metal from these demolition jobs back to the various steelworks in the Midlands. When you got to the steelworks they had these 'checkers' who said whether the load was ok. You'd go in with a load of No1 or No2 steel and the checker would look at it, climb on the load and say yes or no. Within ten seconds the load would be in the furnace and he'd made the decision as to what grade it was! People came up ready to kill the checker but there was nothing they could do. You could go on site with some absolutely brilliant No1 steel and sometimes a checker would refuse it. Then you'd have to

Jim Edwards, driver's mate to Ray Tams, standing beside an S Jones Morris Commercial. *M Jones collection*

ring the yard you'd had it from and they'd get some local guy to copy everything off the note onto his note and take the same steel in and it would be OK. We weren't in a position to do anything about it; we just had to accept it.

Eventually, London Brick decided to use the rail network to transport to cities like Birmingham and we'd be at Small Heath or Winson Green stations to load and transport the bricks to the various building sites. We were lifting them out of railway trucks onto our vehicles. We used to do three loads a day, 5000 bricks, with the help of a mate. They were stacked about thirty-six wide in these railway trucks and you just eased them out, about twelve at a time. You'd flick up the first and the thirteenth and draw them out, drop in your palms and drop on the trailer. We got good at it and worked really fast. We had to put the bottoms and the back wall up and then bang, bang, bang, on they went. That's probably why my knees are no good now because when you got down to the bottom of the truck you'd got to do a knee-bend to pick them up. You were paid by the load so you worked whatever the weather.

Bill Cooper lifting bricks out of trailers at Winson Green station. c1955 Bill Cooper

I worked with some fantastic guys there including Les Marshall, a big, strong guy who drove a Scammell. On that job you needed something that would go across rough ground and he was the only one who could drive this Scammell because he was the only one strong enough; when it went round a corner he had to stand up to steer it. There was also Lofty Goring and Jimmy, John and Tony Peace, three brothers who were all good workers and Gordon Taylor. My brother, Trevor, and my brother in law, Doug Robbins were good blokes too.

At one time we were doing Rank's, the flour mill at Birkenhead, taking wheat up and cattle feed or whatever back. When you loaded there you got no help whatsoever; 200 bags would come down the chute and you'd got to do it quickly because if one got on top of the other it mauled your guts out to get the bottom one out. The blokes there would see you die before they'd give you a lift but we had one driver who always got help. Then he'd take us in to the café and say 'Cup of tea, lads?' He'd get six teas and take a roll of white five pound notes out of his pocket and peel one off to pay for them. He was a character; he'd always got something going on. I remember I had to drive his vehicle once and stopped at a café. I was just getting out of my cab when this bloke comes out with a double-barrel shotgun. 'You've been going around with my wife!' I'm saying, 'No, not me. I've only got this for the day!'

At some stage in the 1960s I mentioned to Frank that I could give him a hand in the office. I used to say to him 'You want somebody in there to give you a lift, Frank. I could come in and do that.' I think I was probably half joking but I'd known him since he first started and we were always good friends. After chivvying him a few times he said 'Right, you can come in here on three months' trial.' So that's what happened and I went in there for £25.00 a week. I was doing general haulage, mostly. The company had all tippers until not long before I went into the office but when John Dickinsons and some other big companies changed over to oil and gas and the steelworks went out of business, we quickly diversified into general haulage.

I remember moaning to Michael (Jones) one day that we could do with some coil-carriers because we weren't really kitted out for it. Anyway, he came into the office that afternoon and said 'Here you are; here's the list.' He'd ordered twenty trailers from Crane Fruehaufs all listed on this piece of paper with the dates, job numbers and everything. That was the sort of people they were; they spent the money on the company. Everybody wanted to work for S Jones because they were the Rolls Royce of companies and paid the top wages. I can honestly say that neither Michael nor his dad ever complained that the men were being paid too much because they knew they earned it. I had the utmost respect for them both; they were fantastic to work for.

The next big step was containerization which we started from scratch, just an old Jones's crane with a jib on that we used to lift the empty containers on. I remember one of the blokes overshooting with the jib once and a container slid on top of Frank Hicken's Zephyr and flattened it!

Then of course there were the tanks. At first we had a couple of sludge gulpers but in the end we had the best tanks you could have carrying anything from orange juice to chemicals to Italy, France, Germany and Holland. About that time we had an agency in Holland and supplied the army on the Rhine with fuel and, at one time, all the major car rallies. We had one or two vehicles on the fuel job all the time; Gypsy Dave and Yo Yo, who died recently, were on this mainly.

The next big thing was Intermodal and we were there right at the start. Tony Sayce initially had the idea to go into this before the Channel Tunnel was finished so he did all the research. When the tunnel opened we were ahead of the game. We bought all the equipment and were the only haulage company at the major European exhibitions.

I retired from S Jones after 51 years in 1996. I don't miss it; you think you're a big wheel at the time but you aren't really. But I have some great memories. Over the years I've worked with some great guys including Peter Sheldon who was my right-hand man in the office, Eric James and Tony Sayce. Eric started the tanks with the sludge gulpers and Tony took over from him. Of course, we had great support from the girls in the office; Sylvia Hall and the girls were the best. Then, of course, Frank Hicken who could do just about anything. He worked all hours of the day or night; he really has been a great guy. I remember his famous words - 'Attention to detail!'

A Jones tanker taken somewhere around Great Barr. Les Cartwright had it from new but didn't drive it very long as he went out to the Middle East. Stan Brindley had it after Les. *Jerry Cooke Collection*

Bill Bunn on the left (owned the garage in Aldridge) with Bill 'Dad' Cooper, 1944/5 with an S Jones Austin.

Vince Cooke collection

An ERF KV 8 wheel tipper. Late 1960s. *Peter Davies*

RIGHT
A petrol Thorneycroft that Bill Cooper drove when he was on the brick job c 1955. This was one of a number that S Jones purchased from Portland Cement. They had autovacs fitted that held half a gallon of petrol. Once, one of the drivers lost his petrol tank going down Hampstead Hill but didn't know because there was enough fuel in the autovac to get him back. They had to send someone out to find the tank which was on the side of the road. *Bill Cooper.*

Jerry Cooke

When I first started at S Jones as a trainee fitter, Bill Cooper's dad was working there on nights servicing the lorries. We all called him Dad Cooper; I can see him now coming to work on his bike. Frank Hicken was the gaffer - if Frank Hicken asked you to do something, you did it! He was a fantastic guy to work for.

In 1977 I went out to the Middle East working for Trans Arabia, Jones's Middle East operation. When they started in the Middle East they had 10 English drivers: Kenny Jillings, Micky Jillings, Bernard Broad, Ernie Hathaway, Billy Clemments, Davey Anslow, Derek Farrington, Stan Brindley, John Matthews and Billy Reynard. John Davies was the mechanic. Billy Smith, who has recently died, was the transport manager with Ken Broster above him. Anyway, Johnny Davies was due for his first leave (you did about four months out there and then came home for three weeks) so I went over as relief mechanic. When he got back I covered for someone else; I think I was out there for about four months the first time. Later on I went back again on a two year contract.

I was only 21 when I first went out and didn't have a clue what to expect as I'd never been out of the country before. When I arrived at Jeddah it was night time and Johnny Davies was there to meet me. He took me to the villa that S Jones rented for us and the next morning I was set to work repairing an ERF 5MW out in the street in the desert heat because at that time there was no covered workshop.

Trans Arabia had an Arab partner who was the sole importer for Imperial Leather, Vosene shampoo and Gold Leaf cigarettes. We used to collect all the containers from the ports and deliver to his warehouses but we also did general haulage for other people. I remember we used to pick yachts up from the port and deliver them all round the Kingdom. They were fantastic boats, worth a fortune. We also carried mobile homes and I remember one of our drivers, Eric Bowers, had got to deliver one of these collapsible homes to a Canadian Mining Company in Kamis Misshat. Anyway, he'd loaded it but couldn't make it secure. We had to do something so in the end I had to weld the sub-frame of the building to the trailer and it had to be cut off when it arrived.

I came back from the Middle East because I got married, but I went out again during the recession of the early 1980s. I did my last stint in 1982/83 and when I came home I went to work in the garage with Les Slymn, the fleet engineer. There were four other mechanics at that time: Tony Peace (Footsie), Stevie Whitehouse, Ian Roberts (Tiny) and Andy Wisdom. We worked in the garage where Jones's is now but then they split the company and we moved further down by the canal. Sometimes, after a day's work in the garage somebody from the Traffic Office would come over and ask if someone could do a night trunk; there was that much work in the late 1980s.

We used to go abroad for breakdowns. One Saturday Paul Clemments phoned me. He always spoke like a growling dog and growled down the phone 'I've lost a wheel off the back of me lorry; the hub and the wheel overtook me!' He told me he was just south of Paris and had a load of hazardous chemicals on. I said, 'Look, I'll get somebody out to you.' I had a book with all the different agents throughout Europe; I still have it, and contacted a garage in Paris to see if they could recover it. That was on the Saturday morning. There was a chap named Alan Perrins who used to have a section of Jones's yard as a breaker's yard so we managed to get an axle from him and the plan was for me and Mickey Boulton to go out and I'd change the axle and Mickey would drive the vehicle back leaving me to drive the brand new Dodge pick-up. So we shipped over to France in the night. On Thursday we arrived at the garage where the vehicle had been taken. I changed the axle and did everything ready to go. Mick got into the lorry and says 'Right, I'm away; I've got a load in the morning and I'll be home tomorrow night.'

The manager of the garage came out to me and said 'Where's the lorry gone?' I told him and he said 'You have not paid for the recovery. You cannot leave here until you have paid.' I told the man that the only security I'd got was the van so he drove it into the garage with all my tools

Jerry working outside on an engine refit in the blistering heat on his first day in Jeddah. The job could have him travelling hundreds of miles on breakdowns. Once, he had to out to go out to one on the Tap Line at Turaif on the Jordanian border with an ERF tractor unit. He couldn't fix it so he put the trailer behind the unit and towed the other ERF on a straight bar for 800 miles to the company's Damman depot.

Jerry Cooke Collection

on and locked the garage doors! So there I am on the outskirts of Paris with nothing, just the clothes I was standing up in. I'd worked hard all day and was absolutely as black as the road but he did finally let me get my bag out of the van and pointed me in the direction of a nearby hotel. It was quite posh and when I said 'Can I have a room for the night?' they weren't keen but they let me stay. I went round to the garage the next day and Jones's had had a bankers' draft couriered so at about 2.00 pm on the Friday afternoon I set off for England. I arrived home about midnight.

It was nothing unusual to be sent out to change a radiator or a diff or put a clutch in - we just did everything on the side of the road. I once went and put a diff in Gordon Taylor's lorry in Oxcroft pit, working in all the mud. I went to Poland to put a piston and liner in when Tommy Whitehouse had broken down the week before Christmas and had come home. I went out with him in the car on 2nd January 1984 and we put the piston and liner in and drove it back.

I remember going out one Monday evening in January, 1985 with Micky Jones, the apprentice, heading for the South of France. We'd loaded a company car with batteries and filters because several of our vehicles were frozen-up in the South of France; in fact, thousands of lorries were stranded out there because the weather was so severe. While we were travelling between Calais and Le Havre we spotted a Beresford vehicle at the side of the road so we stopped to help; we took his filter out and got him going before we got to the first two of ours driven by Roy Brazier and Dave Williams, who were broken down in Le Havre. Anyway, we thawed them out, changed the filters and got them rolling. Then we ran down to Macon where six others were stranded. The drivers were Andy Hood, Mickey Thorpe, Johnny Michelle, Johnny Williams, Chrisie Wright, Paul Clements; all their lorries frozen solid. Anyway, it took about three days to thaw them and get them on their way. We couldn't use a flame so we had to get a tanker discharge pipe and fasten it up the exhaust of one that was running so the warm air would blow on

TOP LEFT
Some of the lads relaxing. Back L-R: Yo Yo, Kenny Jillings.
Front L-R: Ernie Hathaway, Mick Jillings, Stan Brindley.

TOP RIGHT
Billy Clements (L) and Kenny Jillings.

LEFT
1976. Left Mohammed, the kitchen lad and Ali, the
paperwork fixer and chauffeur.

BOTTOM LEFT
Outside the villa in Jeddah L-R: David Hughes, Stan
Brindley, Billy Clements and Bill Reynard.

BOTTOM RIGHT
The first Christmas away. L-R: Bernard Broad, Billy
Clements, Gypsy Dave Anslow, Mick Jillings, Bill Reynard,
Ernie Hathaway, Kenny Jillings and Stan Brindley.
All Jerry Cooke Collection

Bernard Broad (Yo Yo) Jeddah, 1976.
Yo Yo died in 2012. *Jerry Cooke Collection*

to the diesel tank of the other. They were destined for a factory down in Lyon and the best of it was.... they were loaded with TNT! We got back on the Sunday night, we were away nearly a week.

When I left S Jones I worked for myself for about 17 years, doing repairs and running my own lorry. I worked for

One of the boats S Jones had to deliver c1977. As well as the ERF fleet they had Mack 6 wheel, double drives - not popular with the drivers as they were slow. *Jerry Cooke Collection*

Corrs Brewery in Burton on Trent for about 12 years. I now work for Turner's of Hoole. I have a restored ERF in S Jones colours that I take to all the shows.

Vince Cooke

I went to S Jones in 1971. I started off on No.186, a tipper. It was the last of the 150s and had been opened up that much that it was a flier. I went past a Volvo once and the fella driving nearly bit his pipe in two! S Jones had a marvellous system; they had night shift maintenance and your motor had to be greased and checked. When it was time to do it you had to be there. I used to take 186 in and the fitter would say 'we'll tighten everything up' because she used to shake herself loose. She was an LV with wheels right under the cab. I always knew when she was due because when you put a left-hand lock on, the steering wheel went away from you and when you put a right-hand lock on it came back. I'd say, 'She's due, isn't she.' And the fitter would say 'Yeah, she is.'

We had a man named Les Mears who lived out at Nuneaton. It was very rare he came in the yard. If his motor was due we used to swap with him at Nuneaton and take it back to him the next day. S Jones had a wonderful system - ahead of their time.

A story about Frank Hicken the boss at Jones's: A driver rings in 'Frank, Frank, it's on fire!' Frank says, 'What's on fire?' 'The cab!' Frank says 'Get the fire brigade!' The driver says 'Somebody's rung for them. Oh, my god, the roof's fallen in. Oh, my god, the windscreen's smashed out. Oh, my god...' Frank says 'Ring me when it's out, kid.' and put the phone down.

I went off the tippers on to general and then on to tilts doing continental. I did the Continent

Freezing in France, winter 1985. Jerry and Mickey Jones went out to France where several Jones'
vehicles were frozen-up in the severe weather. These three pictures give an idea of the task they faced.
They were away for a week.

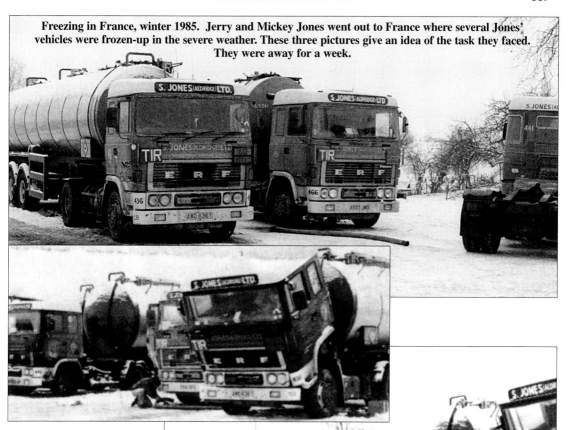

BELOW
Enjoying dinner in France:
L-R: ?, Paul Clements, Andy
Hood, John Michelle, John
Williams, Mick Thorpe, Chris
Wright, Mac Bird (standing),
Jerry and Mickey.
All photos Jerry Cooke.

'Lady Margaret', Vince Cooke's rig. Vince had this on the 4 June 1983, the same day his grandson was born. A cracking lorry, Vince tramped all over Europe in it. Drove it until 1987 when he had S581 YFD.
Jerry Cooke

for 18 years. We had quite a few going overseas at one time. I was the last one; I had a tilt and extendable. I loved every minute of it. We used to meet up with the Beresford boys from Stoke and I remember we were with them coming home from Aosta once and we were at a place called the Monkey House - we called it that because they had a real monkey sitting on the bar. We all had a good night in there; we'd had plenty of 'vino collapso'. Now this place was at the side of a mountain and this particular night we had a new Beresford driver with us. Well, when we all came out this driver says 'I'll be with you in a minute, lads, I'm just going for a weeee.....' He didn't finish his sentence because he'd fallen over the edge. He dropped about thirty feet and we had to get a rope off one of the trailers and pull him up.

Jack Banbury was another Beresford driver I got to know and he told me a story about when he'd landed at Normandy during the war. He was off the beach waiting to advance and just now a convoy comes by and it's the North Staffords. They're all saying 'Eyup, lads' and all that and on one of the trucks was written 'BERLIN OR BUST' and underneath someone had written 'VIA TUNSTALL PLEASE!'

On one trip I was into Calais off the boat and I was supposed to be tipping and loading in Holland. So I filled up with diesel in France. I tipped in Holland and there was a change of plans back to France. Well, I'd got a full tank of diesel but I'd got the DKV ticket and they'd cleared me for tax but this Frenchman wouldn't have it. I suspected he was inebriated and he was quite abusive and insisted I pay the tax. Anyway, I agreed so I could get out of there. He said '71 francs and 19 centimes.' Well, I gave him 71.50 and said there was no change. Straight away he says 'You ask me for change?' I said 'No, I didn't.' Anyway, he says, 'Papers. Passport' and took them from me. 'When you give me 19 centimes you can go.' and promptly put me in a cell. I don't think it helped that I said they'd never forgiven us for winning the war. I told him 'The

Vince in his Willys jeep c 1943 at Whittington Barracks, Lichfield. Vince bought this from Will Gallier of Shrewsbury in 2005 and Will refurbished it for him. Vince Cooke

Germans came in at breakfast time and by the time you lot had finished shaking hands it was all over.' Anyway, at about 3.00 am a young customs man comes in and says 'I think things have improved a little. I think if you apologise now you may be freed.' I said 'Apologise? I'm from Staffordshire. Shut the door on the way out!' I was kept there until the next shift.

In 2009 one of Jones's longest-serving drivers passed away. Dickie Grantham was well-liked and respected by all who knew him and Gypsy Dave and I composed this poem in his memory:

> Richard Grantham
> 'Smiling Dick' our good old mate
> He'd pass us all with his Gardner eight
> When he drove north, east or west, as drivers go
> Dick was the best.
> A good old boy with a beaming smile
> Always happy mile after mile.
> So rest in peace you have earned your rest,
> To your mates and family you were the best.
>   Gypsy Dave and Vinnie Cooke

Graham Griffiths

I worked for S Jones for about 18 years. I remember they took on a sewage job which was running down to Rickmansworth to get this sludge from a sewage bed and bring it back to Brownhills. It used to come up a conveyor straight on to the back of the tipper and we'd take it to Brownhills Pit and tip it straight down the mine shaft. As well as me there was Frank Rothbottom, Billy Brokes, Ivan Baddesley and Dougie Robbins doing the same job. My brother-in-law, Gordon Taylor did one day but he hated it.

On the first outing they did a trial run and Billy Smith was there to make sure everything went OK. Eventually, one of these big tri-axle tippers, loaded with sludge arrived at the pit. Anyway, the back gates on the body proved difficult to open because the pressure had built up but when they did open it gushed out at such a rate that it covered Billy! When you were loaded and pulled away you could feel it coming forward as you changed gear even though there was a baffle in the middle to stabilise it. Ivan Baddesley braked as he came down the A5 one day and it came over the top on to his cab and engine!

During my time with the company I took part in the Lorry Driver of the Year competitions and won the Midland Area finals twice and came second once. I was encouraged by Edward Jones who was interested in all aspects of the job; he was a gentleman, a real old-fashioned transport man.

Sylvia Hall

I started working at S Jones in 1967 doing the wages and purchase ledger but later did some of the personnel work. I could do most things; the only things I couldn't do were to operate a comptometer and shorthand. In those days you all worked together as a team and did what was necessary. Frank Hicken and Bill Smith were in the office when I started; Bill Cooper was still driving at the time. People I remember from my days in the office are Pat Cumpston who sadly passed away, Katie Aplin who was there when I started and Barbara

Sylvia Hall who headed up the team in the office of S Jones.
Sylvia Hall Collection

Beecroft. We got on so well together until we started having youngsters working with us who used to moan if they didn't think they should be doing something. I had to explain that we were just small cogs in a big wheel and if we didn't work together the wheel stopped.

I remember one of the drivers leaving his tipper by the side of the cut without putting the brakes on and it went straight down into the water. It was loaded with turnings and obviously had to be fetched out. We could see it happening from the office but there was nothing we could do.

The fuel pumps were situated alongside the canal and I can remember an incident with Jimmy Pound. He must have forgotten where he was one day because he jumped out of the wagon straight into the water! We had a good laugh.

At the Christmas party one year Mr Edward Jones made a speech. It was a time when the drivers were threatening to go on strike in the New Year and he stood up and spoke directly to the wives telling them how disastrous it would be. Needless to say, it never happened.

Peter Ellis

I was working for Billy Smith's company when we were taken over by S Jones and I stayed with them for 39 years.

At one time we were taking bombs from the Gulf War up to Loch Lomand to the underground storage facility there. We had two teams of five lorries. We were collecting these bombs from bases in England; I think it must have been 1996 because we weren't allowed to use the Erskine Bridge as an oil rig had damaged it so we went through Dunbarton. We had to have police escorts and the first and last lorries had to have a driver and a mate.

Maurice Hill

I worked for S. Jones for 30 years. Before that I worked for Kendricks and Birds. There is a saying amongst drivers about the job: For the first two years every day's a new adventure. Between two and five years it becomes an occupation. After five years, it's a way of life. I think it's true.

Hilltop, West Bromwich. Two pub teams pulling for McMillan Nurses.
Vince Cooke Collection.

Pete Ellis at Felixstowe Docks
1997/8. *Pete Ellis*

ABOVE
The vehicle nearest is EFK 206Y
(Vince Cooke's), the men
standing are L-R: Johnny Links
(Carman), John Shirley, Ernie
Witham and Tommy Whitehouse.
C1985/6 *Vince Cooke*

Vince standing in front of 302.
1975 *Vince Cooke*

Pete Ellis on the cement job. Taken when the vehicle was new, hence the photo. Pete delivered cement for 3 years. S Jones had two of these. *Pete Ellis Collection.*

L-R: Kenny Jellings, Mick Ellis, ?, ?, Bill Clements, ?. In Saudi Arabia. *Mick Ellis*

The lads who delivered the bombs to Scotland take a break. L-R: ?,Mick Hewitt,?,John Tomlinson, *Pete Ellis Collection*

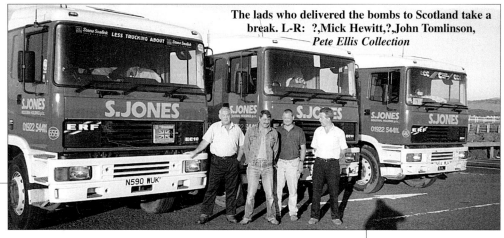

L-R Mick Hewitt, ?, Pete Ellis, Pete Walch, Ray Tucker, John Tomlinson. *Pete Ellis Collection*

ABOVE LEFT
1983 Steve Whitehouse in front of the vehicle driven from new by his father, Tommy, and written off in an accident S of Paris 1988/89 - Tommy was unhurt.
Jerry Cooke Collection

ABOVE RIGHT
Maurice 'Mossa' Hill with his S Jones Truck Rental vehicle, F541 YFD. Dave Lloyd ran F542 YFD.
Maurice Hill

RIGHT
L-R: ?, Basil Hood and Jock Hannah. Jock was driving fleet no 395 when he died at the wheel. Taken in 1980.
Jerry Cooke Collection

RIGHT
The driver of 322 when new was Terry Yeomans. In 1975 Tommy Whitehouse went on the first trip to the Middle East in this but had to abandon it broken down on the Jordanian border. Eric James and Les Slymn went out but their tools were lost in transit so they had to tow it all the way back to the Austrian border where Les repaired it with tools the company had sent out. They were away for several weeks.
Jerry Cooke Collection

ED WEETMAN - Tom Cheadle

Ed, a farmer's son from Fradswell, started working for himself with a Morris Minor pick-up, carting and cutting up logs and selling them. He set up the haulage business in 1967/8 transporting animal feeds from Manchester for Fords of Blythe Bridge. Ed said that when he started one of his first jobs was unloading sacks of sugar beet pulp off a train in Stafford sidings which he'd got to get off and deliver in two days. The problem was there was 100 tons and he was on his own.....but he did it! That was the start of the business.

My brother was one of Ed's first employees; he used to bag shavings for him, but I'd known him since we were teenagers and I went to work for him in 1974. As well as doing animal feeds and sugar beet from the factories around the country we did combines out of Bamfords at Uttoxeter and thermal blocks for a firm in Stafford. I remember we had a couple of blowers working out of CBF at Stone in the early years. Drivers I remember from that time are: Sid Findley, Jim Harmer, David Godwin, Bob Vincent, Peter Davies, Alf Jackson and Alf Baker. The transport Manager was Frank Wragg and the fitters Dave Collett and Paul Oliver. I finished driving in 1982 when Ed went into bulk haulage in a big way. I remember I'd loaded out of King's Lynn one day and when I got back he said he didn't want me driving any more as he needed me in the office because there was so much to do.

Originally, the company was based at Worston Mill, Great Bridgeford (where the restaurant is now) but in 1977 he bought a small transport café at Great Haywood to use as a yard. It was about an acre but he subsequently added to it and the depot, Pasturefields, now stands on nine acres with extensive warehousing and storage facilities. Weetmans is one of the largest bulk haulage operators in the Midlands. I have been a director of the firm for about 10 years and still work full-time. Ed passed away in 2008 and is still sadly missed

Tom standing in front of his Seddon Atkinson with Seddon 400 cab. This was taken in the summer of 76 in Lincolnshire delivering around Weymouth and Poole and bringing fertiliser back up from ICI at Avonmouth.
Tom Cheadle

A Weetman DAF taken on the A500, Junction15 M6
John Heath

A Volvo FH12 Taken at Hanchurch 2007
John Heath

An MAN taken on M6 Stoke, southbound.2007 John Heath

ABOVE
A fleet photo of Volvos taken at
Pasturefields

RIGHT
Ed photographed in the offices at
Pasturefields.

BELOW
A later photo of some of the Weetman
fleet Pasturefields.
All Weetman Collection

STAN ROBINSON (STAFFORD) LTD - Stan Robinson

I was born at Drointon House Farm, Drointon in Staffordshire. My mother was a farmer's daughter, my dad a coal merchant. We lived in several houses in and around Stowe-by- Chartley before settling in Weston where I went to the primary school. My dad had the coal yard at Weston Station; he and his brother were in partnership but he went on his own when I was about eight.

Every day I used to come out of school and instead of going home I'd go to the station yard to find out which village my dad was in and go and find him on my bike - it could have been Stowe, Hixon, Gayton or any of the little villages. My dad had a change of clothes for me in his cab so I'd get out of my school clothes and into my working gear and help him. Sometimes he'd leave a message for me to bag some coke up or something. This was basically what I call my 'seed' in transport because I loved it.

I can remember that as well as doing the coal round Dad collected milk in churns from the local farms. He had five pick-ups: Mrs Earp at Newbuildings Farm, Fred Armitt who was at Bowgage, Deavilles at Grindley down by the station, John Hampson who was just past The Blythe and Edgar Brincliffe. We would pick the churns up, put them on the train at Grindley Station and they'd be in London the next morning.

My dad had an old three ton Bedford that he used to start with a handle - no starter motors in those days! I've now got a two ton Bedford restored in his memory; I wanted a three ton really but couldn't get one. Only one man has criticised it and that was my Uncle John, he said, 'That wonner your dad's wagon, your dad's had got a shorter bonnet!'

I passed my eleven plus and went to Brewood Grammar School as a boarder for four years. When I was fifteen I asked if I could leave - in those days you had to go to sixteen if you went to grammar school- and the Headmaster said he would put it to the governors. When I went back after the Easter holidays he said 'You've got to give a term's notice so you can leave at the end of July. We've come to the decision you'll never earn your living with your head so you might as well earn it with your hands! So I said, 'Thank you very much.'

I left school and went to work for Cooper's Farm at Drointon for six or eight weeks doing general farm work and left to go to work for my uncle, Gil Brown, who had a farm. I was there for two years, living in, driving tractors and hedge-cutting etc. Then we had a row and I left so I went to work for Tom Tavernor who was my mother's brother. Tom had a farm at Weston. I got on well with him; he was like a second dad to me. He'd do a bit of shouting and bawling but when I left he said 'You've been one of the best blokes I've ever had, but I knew I couldna keep you. Your heart went with every wagon that went past.' He was right. All I wanted to do was get out on to the wagons and there on the side of the A51 I saw them all coming through: Dexter's doing London-Liverpool, Fred Rose from Manchester, Buckley's of Warrington, Hunt's of Great Haywood, Beresfords of Tunstall and E R Stocking & Son of Colwich. Actually, John Stocking became my first transport manager years later. He and his dad had two wagons doing Liverpool daily. Then he packed up and eventually came to me; he did 26 years with me before he died.

When I left Uncle Tom I went to Armitage Ware at Rugeley. I was eighteen and a half so I was driving an under-3 ton, four cylinder diesel Morris because in those days you couldn't drive anything heavier if you were under twenty-one. There were three wagons in the area and I applied for this job at Armitage Ware but at first they said they hadn't got a job for me. Then my girlfriend, who is now my wife, asked her sister who worked there to get me an interview with the Personnel Officer. I went for the interview and got the job.

I got married in 1962 and within six weeks there was a job advertised in the paper at H W Hunt's at Great Haywood. I said to the wife 'I'm going to apply for that because they've got a house we could have.' Tom had told me that Johnny Hunt had asked what I was doing because he was looking for a lorry driver. They had three or four houses in the yard and I knew one of them was empty so I rang him up and he said, 'How many bumps have you got on your wagon?' I said, 'None.' Little did he know but six months earlier I'd smashed it up and they'd put a new cab on! I got the job over the phone. He just said, 'When are you going to start?' I started two weeks before I was twenty one so went with his son on a small lorry for a fortnight. Six weeks later he let me have the house which we had to renovate before we could move in. We lived there for six years producing three lovely kids.

I was delivering cattle food for Hunt's, starting off on a four-wheeler then on to an eight-wheeler then a new artic. During my time there I met farmers who became lifelong friends. I left in a hurry when I had a smash and got a job at Richardsons at Rugeley. After being there for six months I bought my first house and moved out of Hunt's to a place in Little Haywood. I was driving an artic all over the country for Richardsons on 'A' licence work which gave me an insight into the other side of the transport job. I was at home one night and saw an advert in the local paper 'Transport Manager/Salesman - Hunt's, Great Haywood'. I applied for the job.

I'd known Eric Pearson for about six years and he came to see me at the house. The interview went like this: 'Write your name and address on there, Stan'. So I did and he said, 'Well, that's legible, when can you start?' That was my interview. When I started I'd got a mortgage, a wife and three kids and I was on £25 a week. This would be at the end of 1969. I also earned extra by going to Richardsons on a Sunday morning for four hours doing repairs. They gave me 10 shillings an hour; that was my beer money.

George Smith had two lorries but one of the drivers had lost his licence. George kept saying to me that I ought to buy his lorry and set up on my own. I mentioned this to Eric Pearson who was my boss at Hunts and he agreed. So I discussed it with my wife on the Monday night and we decided to go for it. BUT we'd got no money. I knew we'd got a life insurance with the Prudential so I asked her how much we were paying and how long we'd paid it for and she told me. The Prudential agent used to go in the local pub every Monday night so I had a look to see if I'd got enough money in my pocket to buy a pint and went down to see Ray, the agent. I said to him, 'How much will I get if I cash this insurance in?' He asked me how much I was paying and for how long, then gave me a quick estimate of £200. My reply to him was 'Cash it in - I'm going on my own!'

I'd got £50 which I was due to pay on the mortgage on the 1st January so I went to the bank for a loan and came out with £800. So that's how I went into business with just £50 of my own money! I bought this second-hand four wheeler Commer with a Perkins P6354 engine off George Smith. On the 1st November 1970 I started on my own. I put the loads together for the Monday and asked Eric Pearson to tell me which one I could have and his reply was 'You're not much of a transport manager if you can't pick your own load!' So I did and I remember that first load was three drops down to Cope's at Longdon: Rookery Farm, Chestall Farm and Horsey Lane Farm. Dan Cope's grandson, Steve Cope, works here now. He came to work for me in the traffic office in 1990 and became a director of the company five years ago.

That was the start of the business, basically. I drove that lorry for eight months before I purchased my first new one. My idea had been to park the four-wheeler up and drive the artic because I could carry more but I soon put the Commer on the road again. So now I had two.

The first driver I set on was Sid Babb; he had the Commer. He worked for me for two or three years. He was a big, rough bloke but with a heart of gold. He was OK while there was just two or three of us but once we got to six or seven of us he couldn't hack it so he left. I'd known him since he was young when I was delivering coal to his mum and dad. I remember when he came for the interview he'd got a nice suit and tie on and that's the only time I ever saw him dressed up. He worked hard for me; I was driving the artic and he was driving the four-wheeler.

To start with we were operating from the back garden of our house, Chase View, Little Haywood. When we bought the house there was a building site behind it and our house, which was in a row, had a very long garden that had a road by it. I made a road in on my back garden with brick-ends and I used to park the van alongside the lorry. When we got the second lorry I rented Colwich Station yard which is just under the railway bridge on the left. I moved in there with the four-wheeler, the artic and three trailers.

Stan's gran, who kept the Cock Inn at Stowe by Chartley, ran a local bus service (Uttoxeter, Gayton, Stafford) and also had a licence for tours and excursions to places like Blackpool and Alton Towers. Stan's dad used to drive the bus sometimes. This would be in the 1930s. *Hixon History Society*

Sid was driving the four-wheeler one day and I was driving the artic when my wife was taken ill. It was a Saturday morning and we'd both got loads on to deliver and we'd also got a trailer dropped at a farm to tip as well. While I was out delivering the first load my daughter rang up to say my wife was very ill so I came back home and brought half the load back with me. I parked up outside the house. When Sid came back he said 'What's up?' Anyway, he parked his lorry in the yard and came back up to the house and picked my lorry up. I said 'Just take it down the yard and dump it.' He said 'No, I'll go and deliver it.' He hadn't got an artic licence but off he went. At about 8 o clock that night I was getting my wife off to the hospital when this wagon pulls up and I thought that's the trailer we've got at the farm. He'd gone and delivered my load, gone up to this farm and the trailer was sunk in the ground and he'd unloaded 20 ton of beet pulp on his own, got the trailer up and brought it back. As I say, he hadn't even got a Class 1 licence. That was the sort of man he was; he'd say 'I'll get it done, Stan. You leave it with me.' He was a grand lad, he was, but that's life.

ABOVE
A Stan Robinson Foden
*Photographed by John
Heath on the M6 at Carlisle
in 2007*

This office photo was taken
when Chris Castell was
going on maternity leave -
her daughter is now 15.
L-R back:
Ann Irving, Joyce Talbot,
Flo Robinson. Front: L-R
Val Plant, Chris Castell, Liz
Waterfall, Pauline Wilson.
Robinson Collection

Stan with his wife and children:
L-R Ian, Flo, Stan, Mark and
Pauline.
Robinson Collection

A fleet photo taken in the yard in 1994. Robinson Collection

Over the next two or three years we built up to about 4 artics and 2 rigids and in about 1977 we bought W Davies & Co at Stafford, a well-established company with 10 lorries. They did work for Evode, Universal, GEC, Dormans and other Stafford companies. I was Transport Manager and doing the office work along with Doris, a woman who helped and my wife was doing the wages. I've always said that my wife has been a pair of reins to me; kept me in check, kept me in order. Behind every good man is a good woman.

We started doing trunks with a company in Scotland, Peter Laing Carriers. We bought them out in about 1992 and started a Scotch depot. I can remember coming back and we'd got 40 vehicles and they'd got 20 and saying to the wife 'That makes us 60, that'll do.' Now 20 years later we've got 180 plus.

We moved to where we are now in about 1977 purchasing 2.5 acres. We had about fifteen lorries by this time. Not long after we moved here we nearly went bust because we were running a lot of artics and no four wheelers. I was doing all the traffic myself at this time and had got a couple of seven and a half tonners in the fleet. I can remember that one of the artics would come out of London with 20 ton of coils on and would be paying about £100 to Birmingham and a little seven and half tonner did three or four pick ups in London, brought them back, dropped and earned £200. I thought there's something wrong here so I started ringing people up and saying 'Have you got any bits and pieces you can't deal with' and they'd say 'I've a pallet for here and a pallet for there.' I used to have a sheet of A3 paper and I'd just write Scotland at the top and Cornwall at the bottom and as I got the work I'd make loads up. That's how it worked but it's all done on computer now. All very different now; the fun's gone out of it. I'm glad I'm coming out instead of going in because we've had the good times.

I have a daughter, Pauline, and two sons, Mark and Ian. I also have two grandsons and six granddaughters. All three of my children work in the business along with my eldest grandson and three granddaughters.

I can remember when I bought this depot John Stocking said 'You'll never fill this yard, Stan.' You should see it on a Saturday afternoon now!

Keith Berkshire

Stan started roughly the same time as me at Armitage Ware. I went driving at first but have also worked in the mould-making department. When Stan started he was driving what we used to call the 'Tiddler'. Tommy Lewis had to go on to a seven tonner so Stan could have it.

Keith Berkshire with Leyland DAF taken at Armitage loading bay. 1980s *K Berkshire Collection*

When we went down to London we had to use the A5 which meant going up Kilsby Bank. When you got to this bank you couldn't get a run at it or anything because it went up that sharp. Well, the Tiddler was always overloaded and Stan used to lift the bonnet up and put Easy Start on so it would give him more power. He used to do his work and he'd come into the digs in Norwich Road, Forest Gate and he'd be as black as anything from the smoke off the engine.

He was a good, hard working lad. In the morning, if he was going early, he'd have about six eggs and he'd do them himself because the landlady, Ma, didn't start 'til about seven. I can see him now boiling these eggs. We used to have to wear boiler suits at Armitage and I remember Stan used to wear his belt over the top of his and he used to pull this belt that tight around his waist - it was just as if he'd ratcheted it up! I worked for Armitage for about 38 years before retiring in 1996.

Tom Lewis

I started at Armitage Ware in 1957 so I'd been there a few years when Stan came. I actually started in the garage but I had a row with the foreman. I was spraying a van at the time and and I turned the spray gun on him so they suspended me for two weeks. Wilf Booth came down to see me and said, 'You and Keith Brentnall are never going to get on so how do you fancy going driving?' Anyway, I gave it a try and I had the Tiddler (490 KRE) that Stan had. I came in one Friday night and the boss says, 'Empty your wagon we've got a new driver going on that and he can't drive the big ones yet. You can have the Thorneycroft'. The new driver was Stan and I went with him in the Tiddler for three or four days to show him the ropes. I forget now where we went; it could have been Derby and probably a night out in Leeds. The following week he was on his own.

I remember we were coming out of Bournemouth one day and we were coming up this side of Salisbury. Anyway, Stan gets a puncture by Larkhill Camp - he had a lot of punctures because the Tiddler was always overloaded - so we pulled over and his spare was flat. His wheels were smaller than mine so I couldn't help. Anyway, Stan walks back to me with his case and puts it in the wagon. I said 'What are you doin'?' He says 'I'm going home; I'm taking Florrie to the pictures tonight!' Years later I was at Uttoxeter Truck Show and Stan was there and we were talking. I said 'Do you remember when you left the Tiddler down at Salisbury? What would you do if any of your drivers did that?' 'I'd sack 'em.' We both laughed.

At Armitage we carried toilets, wash hand basins, cast iron baths as well as clay back from Corfe Castle or Redruth in Cornwall and flint stones from Sandwich or Shoreham. We used to go up to Liverpool docks with washbasins upside down, five in a crate, and I've seen Stan lift them off the side of the wagon straight on to the stack. Nobody else did that; he was very strong. When he left Armitage he went to Hunt's. Numerous times I've been going down to Cornwall, having left at 5.00 am and Stan's been coming out of Bristol with his first load. He used to do two a day; he'd go down at midnight and load up and then back to do another one in the afternoon.

The people I can remember who were there the same time as Stan were Dick Beddows, Eric Ridley and Ernie Wainwright. Ernie and Stan were big pals. Ernie was a big, strong chap who died when he was only 39. I was one of his coffin bearers with Stan, Billy Littler and Eric Ridley.

I remember Stan had me driving all the way along Liverpool docks down to Toxteth one day so he could take a photo of the name of a ship - 'The Floristan'. We went in my wagon and drove from one end to the other so he could take this picture. I don't know whether he kept it.

When he first came to Armitage Ware I can't remember whether he came on a push bike or a motorbike but not long after he started he bought a Ford van. One Saturday he used the garage to do the brakes on this van. He put new brake shoes on it and pushed the cylinders in and of course when you've done that you've got to pump the brakes. Well, he went screaming across the forecourt and put his foot on the brakes straight to the floor. He went through a wrought iron fence and ended up in the lane and, of course, the front of this van was all smashed in.

When he first went on his own he had a Commer with a 6354 Perkins in and he came to our house one night and said, 'The engine's stopped!' I said 'What's up with it?' 'I don't know; I've had it towed home.' He lived at Haywood at the time. Anyway, it was winter and we got a tarpaulin sheet over the cab and made a tent and stripped the front out. It was the timing gear that had sheared so I drove the pin out and got a new one. We worked until about 2.00 or 3.00 in the morning. I'd got to be at Armitage Ware by about 6.00 am and he was going out at 5.00am to deliver his load. He'd probably do two loads that day! When I saw Stan at Uttoxeter he said 'Who'd have thought when we were fixing that Commer all those years ago that the business would snowball like it has.'

A couple of BMCs and a Commer at Boathouse Lane loading bays. c1963
Tom Lewis Collection

I'd worked for Armitage for just short of 40 years when they made me redundant but after two weeks I was back there on agency work. A few months later they put me on nights and I decided to finish.

Tom snapped with one of his classic cars a 1967 Volvo Amazon. c1992.
Tom Lewis Collection

A Rogerson horse and cart - one of approximately 30 horses at the turn of the century. *Rogerson Collection*

L-R Harry Rogerson with Joseph and Fred taken at Colwyn Bay 1940s *Rogerson Collection*

J ROGERSON (COBRIDGE) LIMITED - Joseph Alan Rogerson

The business of furniture removing, carting and coal dealing was started in 1885 by 45 year old Joseph Rogerson, my great grandfather. About four years later he was joined by his eldest son, also Joseph and eventually by his two younger sons, William and Frederick.

The first job of any importance was for Corn and Sons of Top Bridge Works, Longport which later became Richards Tiles of Tunstall. Rogersons was originally based in Dale Street, Burslem but after a couple of years moved to Navigation Road. By 1901 the business had increased to 35 horses and carts and two large furniture vans. My uncle used to tell us that the runaway furniture van in *The Card* by Arnold Bennett was based on a real-life incident involving one of Rogersons' vans. Joseph Sr. died as a result of an industrial accident in 1901 when a boiler he was supervising exploded - see extracts from *The Sentinel* below.

By 1909 the business was being run by Joseph Jr (my grandfather), and William and Frederick, and a funeral undertaking business was formed under the name of W & F Rogerson. Joseph joined the army in 1914 for the First World War and served in the Veterinary Corps using his knowledge and love of horses. He was demobbed in 1919 with a full disability pension and came back into the business.

The first motor vehicles, two AEC lorries, were purchased in 1918. In about 1919 the firm started to operate buses at Burgess Street, Middleport. The routes included Tunstall-Longton, Burslem-Newcastle, Newcastle-Market Drayton (via Ashley), Hanley-Newcastle (via Basford Bank).

Joseph and his family moved to Hot Lane, Burslem in 1923 and his sons Frederick, Joseph and Harry (my father) worked from there. By 1927 the business had moved to Leek New Road, Cobridge. The front garage was built approximately two years later with additional land being purchased over several years. In 1928 the buses were sold to the Potteries Electric Traction Co (later PMT), and the funeral business comprising six black horses and a large Wolsley car were sold to the Burslem Co-operative Society. William and Frederick virtually retired leaving Joseph and his sons to carry on with the road haulage side of the business.

VT27 Leyland PLSC3 Lion bus, new to Rogerson's in 1928. The Potteries Electric Traction Co took over W & F Rogersons in the same year. The fleet at that time included Leyland, Dennis, Albion and Karrier vehicles, 19 in total although it is believed they had about 26 vehicles at one time. *Martin Hearson Collection.*

One of the biggest jobs was in 1933 when the company helped with the excavations for The Arcade in Hanley (subsequently Lewis's) working with the first mechanical digger in the area.

In September 1950 the Labour government nationalized the business taking five long-distance vehicles. This left us with six vehicles restricted to a 25 mile radius. The same year my grandfather died leaving the business to Frederick, Joseph and Harry. I joined the company in April 1955. The last of the horses working the Middleport Mills finished in 1956.

At its height the business had approximately 25-30 vehicles. About half the lorries worked on long distance mainly for the pottery industry - we did a lot of work for Royal Doulton delivering to London stores including Selfridges and Harrods. Return loads were flint for the pot banks and fruit and veg from Covent Garden, Birmingham and Liverpool Docks to local fruit and veg firms.

We also acquired several contracts with the NCB delivering huge quantities of coal to local schools, hospitals and power stations. We delivered millions of bricks from Wilkinson Brothers, High Lane to Sheffield which were used to build the first high-rise flats in Sheffield. In 1973 we started working for Wades of Burslem delivering to whisky distilleries in Scotland. The tippers mainly worked on the local gas works, coal haulage and the City Council.

Drivers who achieved long service with us include Alf Lawton (over 50 years); Harold Lawton, George Pettit, Billy Jebb, Jim Ellis, Bert Bloor and Tommy Deakin (all over 30 years); and Peter Bamford and Gerry Wright (over 20 years).

My father died in 1980, Frederick in 1991 and Joseph Jr in 1999. I ran the business until it was sold to H & H Commercials in 1997. I continued to work under H & H Commercials until my retirement in 2003.

Extracts from The Evening Sentinel Monday 7 October 1901

BOILER EXPLOSION AT BURSLEM
TWO KILLED; FOUR PERSONS INJURED

A boiler explosion occurred with disastrous results at Burslem on Saturday evening. The affair happened on the premises of Messrs J Rogerson & Son, carters and furniture removers, in Navigation Road and caused the instantaneous death of a child and shocking injuries to five other persons.

The boiler was of the vertical type, and was used for driving a steam engine supplying the motive power to a chaff cutting machine. It stood uncovered in an open yard of the stables tenanted by the firm and situated a short distance from Mr Rogerson's residence. On Saturday the boiler was in use and about 5.30 Mr Joseph Rogerson was superintending the working of the machine preparing fodder. At that time there were several children playing in the immediate neighbourhood and Mr Rogerson was assisted by a carter named William Walker and others. While they were engaged two terrific reports were heard and the huge boiler, which is over two tons in weight, was seen sailing bodily through the air right over the adjoining houses in the direction of Lower Hadderidge. There the boiler struck the frontage of the Cross Keys public house, damaging the spouting and wall, and the force of the impact being so great as to throw a piano in the room from one side to the other.

The alarm thus occasioned was intensified when the boiler, falling into the roadway caused a fracture in a four inch water main some feet below the surface. Through the break the water escaped with force flooding the street. The Waterworks Company's employees had to be requisitioned to make good the main and they were engaged until a late hour. In the fall the cumbersome mass toppled over, crushing beneath its terrible weight a little child named Annie Hodgkinson, aged seven years, the daughter of Thomas and Sarah Hodgkinson living at 34 Amicable Street. The unfortunate child was playing with other youngsters and the boiler's weight pinned her to the road, mutilating her to a shocking degree, particularly about the head. Her death was instantaneous. Many children had been playing in the street and some who had only just been sent for by their parents had a very narrow escape.

The noise of the explosion was heard for some considerable distance and created great excitement and alarm. There was a wild rush to the scene and a frightful spectacle presented itself to the large crowd that had gathered. Besides the death of little Annie Hodgkinson, the explosion had resulted in shocking injuries to five persons. These were: Mr Joseph Rogerson, aged 64, who had a fractured leg and severe bruises about his body. Arthur Rogerson aged 10, his son, who was shockingly scalded on the face and body. Frederick Rogerson, aged $2^{1}/2$ years (a grandchild of Mr Rogerson) who was severely cut about the face and so badly scalded that his recovery was not expected to survive. William Walker, 37, Lower Hadderidge, carter, scalded on the legs and sustained a cut penetrating to the bone. A child named Tideswell who escaped with slight injuries to the face..

The article goes on to describe how the police and medical staff handled the situation and ends:

What caused the explosion had not at the time of writing been ascertained. The boiler's connection with the engine was a small pipe protruding from the stable wall. This, of course, was snapped when the boiler was lifted from the yard. The only visible damage to the boiler as it lay in Lower Hadderidge was a large indentation at the top, with a jagged hole. Whether or not the explosion was caused through a deficiency of water was not known. Indeed, on the contrary, it was stated there had been the necessary quantity of water within the boiler. As the boiler stood uncovered in the stable yard there was little destruction on the premises. The only damage consisted of the removal of two stable doors. It was stated that the boiler was being worked at a pressure of 55lb and that just before the accident it was examined and was thought to be all right.

A second death occurred on Sunday morning, when little Frederick Rogerson, the grandchild of Mr Rogerson succumbed to the injuries he received. The boy, who was removed to the hospital in a precarious condition, lingered in agony until 7.00 am yesterday, when he died. The other victims are progressing favourably.

Joseph Rogerson died as a result of his injuries two weeks later.

27A Foden Alpha 3000 with caterpillar C12, 400 bhp engine. Taken in 2001 at Land Recovery in Alsager.
Rogerson Collection

Harold Lawton and his wife celebrating their silver wedding anniversary. L-R: Mrs Lawton, ?, Harold.   Harold worked for Rogersons for over 30 years. In 1969 his lorry was in a collision at Wolsley Bridge when he was fatally injured. *Tony Lawton*

BELOW
Rogerson drivers and vehicles at Johnson Matthey, Kidsgrove with what was then (1963) the largest single colour overseas order - final destination Russia on 3 six wheelers, 1 four wheeler and a J. Matthey four wheeler to Hull Docks. L-R Harry Rogerson, Johnson Matthey employee, Lester Bishop, Alan Rogerson, Jimmy Ellis, Gordon Machin with Tommy Deakin in the cab. *Deakin Collection*

Alan's retirement in January 2003. L-R Sharon Jones, Alan, Sue Williams and Carol Lawton. *Rogerson Collection*

Bill Jebb

I first started driving when I was eight in a field near Bagnall village driving a Chevrolet, reg: VT 6009. My father worked for Mr Lord of Bagnall Hall and one day we were in this field by the hospital getting the hay in and my father said 'You can drive while Mr Lord is rowing up and I'll get on the wagon to load up.' So I had a go and I stalled it. My father climbed down off the load and he got the starting handle and wound it. When he'd got it going again he said 'Don't you stall it again or you're off!' Well, I didn't; I just drove it steadily around the field until the load was finished. That started my fascination with driving.

I left school at 14 but started driving when I was 21 for my brother-in-law, Ron Mear of Lane Head Farm, Endon. I was driving an ex-War Department petrol Albion. Sometimes I'd go to Burton on Trent to pick up a load of grains for cattle fodder. I used to have to roll this Albion down Holehouse Lane to get it going and then put the handbrake on and place a brick on the accelerator to keep the engine revving. Then I'd jump out and go round to the front to push the choke in because it was at the side of the radiator, then run back round, move the brick and jump in. I'd do two trips to Burton on Trent and I used to take half a dozen eggs for them because in the summer they'd give me half a pint of beer. It was thirsty work because I had to load it myself with a big fork or shovel out of railway trucks so I was grateful for the beer! When I got back I'd be delivering to farms around Biddulph Moor and Lask Edge.

In April 1967 I started working for Rogersons driving a Morris four wheel tipper. We used to go down to the Gas Works at Etruria and pick a load of coke up and take it to Stafford 16 MU. We'd stockpile it there and they'd load you up again to take it round to different units on the Camp. At the end of the day you'd come back empty. This lorry had belonged to Fox's who were based on Sneyd Hill. Later I got promoted to a six wheel tipper, an AEC Marshall which

The first lorry Bill drove aged 8 at Bagnall Hall Farm - a Chevrolet. L-R: Bill, Christine Lord, Lassie, Wilfred Lord, Bill's dad, William, on top

George Pettit had driven from new - OEH797K. George had every new lorry Rogersons had.

An Albion petrol flat, used on the farm after being involved in a head-on crash at Baddeley Green in Dec 1953. Bill is the young man on the back of the trailer.

At one time most of Rogersons' vehicles were drop-sided. In the mornings I'd do coal and then when I got back to the depot at night it was take all the sideboards off so the tipper would then be a flatbed. At 7.00 am I'd go down to The Michelin and put steel drums on to take to Dunlop in Birmingham and bring empties back.

Rogersons had about 25 vehicles on the road when I started - tippers and flats. Alan's father, Harry, was in charge of the garage and transport. Fred worked in the office with old Joe. Cissie and Polly were sometimes in the office. They were a very nice family.

I finished when I was 59 in 1992 because I had a blood clot on my brain. I was in Blackpool with my wife and we were crossing the road and I said, 'Hold on a minute there's a Century Oils wagon coming.' Miriam said, 'You won't know who's driving that out here.' Anyway, when it came nearer the driver shouts 'Eyup, Bill.' It was John Underwood from Cobridge. I started to walk down this street and I collapsed and was rushed to the Victoria Hospital in Blackpool. Anyway, my driving days were finished as nobody would set me on because of insurance. I've been finished for 20 years now.

Another firm I remember from my time as a driver was Baggeley and Bloors who were based opposite Rogersons. They did a lot of pot-bank work carrying swath, that sort of thing. They had tippers so a diesel loading shovel on rubber tyres would load them.

Then there was Hancocks who were just past the lights heading for Burslem on Nile Street who ran 4 red Dodges - 2 tippers and 2 flats. Fred and Harry bought all four; John from Chesterton drove the long wheelbase with sideboards (DBF 49H) and the late Frank Wrench drove the AEC flatbed (MEH 970K) although I drove both these at times. I drove FVT 682J which was a Dodge 4 wheeler and I was driving this through Lichfield one day when a lady driver had a blackout; she came out of a side road and drove under my vehicle. She was very badly injured but still living. The car was a write-off. That was on the 17th October 1974. Luckily for me I had a witness, a man from Burton.

Another accident I had was when I was driving a Seddon 4 wheel tipper BLG 628F. I was driving back to the depot empty and climbing Kidsgrove Bank. A lorry from Ireland skidded in the snow and crashed into me. My vehicle was pushed over an 11ft pavement and through a stone wall. I was trapped in the cab for about half an hour before Blue Watch got me out. I remember a double decker bus came up while I was waiting for help and the driver got out and gave me his PMT coat to keep me warm - he threw it through the windscreen which was smashed in. Luckily I wasn't badly injured and the ambulance that took

Bill's Seddon after accident on Kidsgrove Bank in 1971

me to hospital waited for me and brought me home. Alan (Rogerson) was at a football match at Blackburn at the time and later came to see me at home. I was bruised from head to toe, all my teeth were broken and there was still glass in my hair. Some months later I was having difficulty eating and I discovered there was a piece of tooth still lodged in my gum!

Bill taken by Ros Unwin 2012

In all the years I've been driving I have never been booked; I've always had a clean licence. Some of the drivers I remember from Rogersons are George Pettit, Jerry Wright, Jimmy Ellis and Tommy Deakin, Bill Bradbury, the late Alf Lawton and his brother Harold.

A Rogerson Ford taken in Newbury
in August 1990

RIGHT
Bill on his way to Hereford with a
load of coke destined for a school.
No sheets in those days!

LEFT
A Rogerson Guy Big J with double-drive axles.

BELOW
26 March 1991, Bill towing Jim Ball's Leyland back
to Cobridge from Lockerbie. They were stopped by
the police and made to go back 5 miles while they
tried to work out if they were over the legal weight or
not! In the end they were allowed to continue.
All photos unless otherwise stated Bill Jebb

ARTHUR WEDGWOOD, COBRIDGE   Philip Wedgwood

My granddad, Arthur started the transport business in 1905 in Cobridge alongside the family boiler making business. Ultimately Granddad was to end up running the boiler works as well as the transport business. His first vehicles were probably two Straker steam buses. The family lived in Podmore Street, Burslem where my father, Stanley, was born in 1907. The company probably finished in the late 1920s.

Our firm did quite a lot of furniture removal work, sometimes working with Richard Howle (R D Howle, Red Street, Chesterton). On one occasion uncle Arthur and his Uncle Jos were running light towing a van trailer. Coming to a long descent the usual out of gear operation was performed. At the bottom there was a bend in the road and after putting the wagon back into gear it didn't seem to be pulling very well. As Arthur was puzzling about this, out of the corner of his eye he spotted something white. Looking over his shoulder he then saw it was the white painted roof of the van. This van was on its side but still attached to the tow bar. He got down and went to the back doors, a little apprehensively because one of his uncles was travelling in the van. Looking inside, at first he could only see the pile of sacking that was used to wrap the furniture. Then the pile began to heave and eventually his uncle appeared, with the comment 'Eee Arthur that were a light-yeaded trick!'

The second hand five ton Foden steamer at Corkscrew Bank between Endon and Leek loaded with an industrial loco from Cauldon Lowe.
Philip Wedgwood Collection

The N S Railway had quarries at Cauldon Lowe which operated with three industrial locos: Frog, Toad and Bobs. Granddad had the contract to bring them, one at a time, to the NSR Stoke Works for overhaul. He used a second hand five ton Foden steamer (M6131 new to Jenners' of Edinburgh). Imagine doing that double journey three times with a vehicle severely overloaded and some tremendous hills, not least Ladderedge. This photo was taken on Corkscrew Bank, between Endon and Leek, at the section of the main road which is now by-passed by the cutting.

With the exception of a 6 ton Foden bought in 1924, Granddad only ever operated second hand vehicles which included two traction engines (a Marshall and a Foden). There came a time when two five tonners lay in the yard; one with a broken chassis and the other with a broken

Unloaded and already on the ferry - note the time on the Liver Building clock - 6.20am.
Philip Wedgwood Collection

crankshaft. Arthur Jr (my uncle) had the idea of making an artic. He shortened the chassis of M248, making a tractor unit and made the trailer from the chassis of M6131. He took it to Foden's for them to fit the fifth wheel and paint it. Everything else he did himself. It was used to take Twyford's products to Liverpool docks where he crossed on the Wallasey ferry to Ellesmere Port. There he picked up a load of cement to bring back to the Michelin site when it was being built. This would mean leaving Cobridge at 2.00 am having loaded the night before. In the photo on the ferry you can see the time on the Liver Building clock 6.20 (a.m.) and he's already unloaded and on his way to Ellesmere Port. Returning to Stoke and loading for the outward trip again they would be in bed about midnight getting two hours sleep before setting out again.

One of Philip's restored vehicles, a 1934 Sentinel type S4 steam wagon. Philip and his late brother, Dennis, restored it between 1982 and 1993.
Philip Wedgwood

THE FODEN SOCIETY Kevin Upson

Fodens of Elworth, Sandbach can trace its history back to 1856 when a young Edwin Foden from nearby Smallwood joined agricultural engineers, Plant and Hancock at Elworth foundry. Edwin soon became a partner in the company and in 1887 it became E Foden Sons and Company, and later Fodens Limited.

Fodens initially built steam traction engines and agricultural equipment but from 1915 onwards concentrated on steam wagons. They were widely regarded as the finest available and many were exported. From 1932 the company moved to diesel power and with the DG (Diesel-Gardner) range from

Edwin Foden

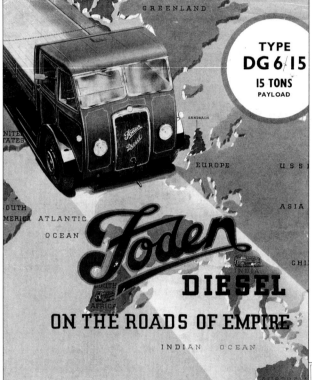

1937 developed an enviable reputation as 'the Rolls Royce of trucks'.

During the 1940s Fodens built Crusader tanks alongside lorries and shell casings for the war effort. After the war, Fodens introduced their much improved FG range and reigned supreme in road transport until the 1970s when they built a new state-of-the-art assembly plant next to the old Elworth Works. The downturn came and in 1980 - Fodens called in the Receiver. Their assets were bought by North American truck manufacturer, Paccar. Production of Foden lorries continued at Elworth until 2001 when it was moved to the Leyland Trucks facility, by then also owned by Paccar. In 2005 Paccar needed the production space for its DAF models and announced it was to

Some promotional material for the Foden DG6/15

Four generations of the Foden family with *The Pride of Edwin* a 1916 5 ton overtype steam wagon.

L-R: 'J.E' Foden, Billy Foden, Reg Foden, David (son of JE), Christopher.

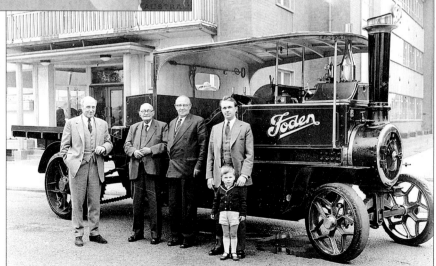

'retire' the Foden marque. The last Foden lorry was built at Leyland in July 2006. This was Fodens' 150th anniversary year and they could legitimately claim to have been the world's oldest truck manufacturer.

The Foden Society was founded in 1992 by Gary Grysa, a Foden owner and enthusiast, and myself. I had worked at Fodens and also owned a historic Foden vehicle. The Society has around 450 members worldwide, including people from the truck, bus and steam preservation movement as well as many current and former Foden users. The Annual General Meeting is held in Sandbach every autumn.

In 2012 the Foden Society part-financed a project by a group of members and ex-employees to place a permanent memorial at the site of Elworth Works. A block of limestone, quarried in Derbyshire, was duly brought by a Foden lorry to the site of the former main entrance on Middlewich Road. It was unveiled on 6th March, 2012 by William Foden, former Chief Executive of Fodens Limited and great-grandson of the founder.

The Foden Society operates a website at www.thefodensociety.org.uk - where news, pictures and membership details can be found.

The last Foden to be built at Leyland. 2006

Unveiling of the memorial stone 2012.
Back L-R: Robert Foden, Allan Littlemore, Bill Foden, Kitty Foden, Christopher Foden.
Front Hugh Foden and Kitty's daughter.

Foden Twinload in Sandbach town centre. All photos The Foden Society Collection.

THE GALLERY

A few more that we just couldn't fit in the main book

Thorneycroft Sturdy of C Knight & Sons Limited with driver and porter for removals.
Carl Johnson Collection

ERF C1561 of Mrs Smith, Station Garage, Kidsgrove on the Brooke Bond Tea contract.
Carl Johnson Collection

Specially constructed vessels coming into the steel works at Shelton from Distington Engineering, Cumbria.
Ken Smith

ABOVE
Jack Haydon of Biddulph
standing in front of his
Albion cattle wagon. Jack
started the firm in 1918. The
driver is the first man he
employed, Dick Copeland.
Jack's son, Fred still lives in
Biddulph.
Fred Haydon

RIGHT
ERF CI of Checkley
Transport, photographed at G
D Allens yard, Lower Tean.
Carl Johnson Collection

One of Nixons of Wolstanton.
John Heath Collection

The Trentham Gravel fleet taken at Imperial Garage Hanford, now a Stobart depot. A solitary ERF along with Reo Speedwagons and other unidentified vehicles. 1930s. *Carl Johnson Collection*

A Bedford OW on right and newer Bedford O Type. These were used on a coal round but Jim Booth later went on to Bibby's Corn with a Commer 2-stroke. *Carl Johnson Collection*

A Harts of Biddulph line-up - Commer 2 strokes. They started in 1930 as coal merchants. They ran mostly Bedfords and Fords. Alan Hart remembers hauling ex RAF aircraft for a Warrington company that scrapped them, and once a Dakota fuselage to London Docks. Some Harts drivers: John Mellor, Frank Mellor, Jim Malloy, Eric Bradbury, Tom Wilshaw, Dennis Rowley, Arthur Boon, Bill Wilbraham, George Lonstreath, Russ Horton, Eric Armet, Joe Brassey. *Eric Rogers*

These pictures are Stan Jukes's taken in 1974/5.

This is the first Laverda M152 to arrive in England by
road prior to this they all came by train.
Stan at the wheel.

As above

This is a load of pea
harvesters from a firm
called Kuhne Agmcole
Machines from Saverrne
in Eastern France.
These were marketed by
Bamford Agricultural
Machinery of Uttoxeter.

The next two pages are from John Heath's extensive collection of photographs taken when he was driving for Beresfords and for Plants of Crewe - not strictly a Staffs haulier but within spitting distance. The next three pictures are when John was stranded at Aosta when the Customs officers went on strike.
L-R: ?, Stan Jukes, Tommy (Smiths of Eccles) ?,?, John Heath.

RIGHT
As above

ABOVE
L-R: Stan Jukes, John Durber. The two Atkinsons are Beresford vehicles.

RIGHT
Ken Beresford with three of his old drivers at Sandbach Festival of Transport, 2012. L-R: Stan Jukes, Ken, Pete Stevenson and John Heath.

John's ERF, H954 KEH on the M62, Juct. 24 after it had been rammed from behind by a Scania when he was stopped in traffic. The driver of the Scania had to be cut out of the cab which took two and a half hours. John was shaken but not seriously hurt although one person died in the accident. 1992

RIGHT: As above

BELOW LEFT: Gordon Plant, one of the old haulage men sadly missed.

BELOW RIGHT
This picture of John with his ERF was taken at Gordon Plant's farm near. Nantwich. John, a keen photographer and active member of REVS, is now in his 70th year; he goes to all the major shows armed with his camera!

**Richard Cresswell line-up of his restored AECs A
Mustang, a Mammoth Major and a Mercury.
Taken a few years ago at Woollaton Park.**
R Cresswell Collection

Taken in a layby in France when Alan Shaw and fellow drivers were
bringing Dodgems to a Prestatyn fairground. L-R: Graham ?, Alan, John
Lovatt and Frank Breeze with a Leyland Marathon purchased from BRS.
A Road Boss at the far end of the line-up was one of the first in the country.
Morgans actually had the first bonneted White Road Boss over here.
Photo mid 1970s. A Shaw

John Fowler's
Milton smash. John
lost control coming
down to Milton
crossroads in his ex-
Whitbread Dennis
Pax V. Luckily, no-
one was hurt. Mid
1970s. Sadly, John
is no longer with us.
A Mason

This picture of one of Kettles was taken in the late 70s/early 80s when about 10 drivers worked away for several weeks when the Brecon bypass was under construction. Joe Dulson standing by the vehicle. *Paul Dulson Collection*

Maurice Hill (left) with Fred Foster who later had his own tipping business. Taken at Cheslyn Hay, the vehicle is a Guy Big J. *maurice Hill Collection*

ABOVE
Terry Bellamy in his Leyland Mixer at Hulland Gravel, Freehay. Terry did 36 years first as a driver and later Plant Maintenance Supervisor before retiring in 2007.
T. Bellamy

RIGHT
Bernard Broad (Yo Yo) driving a Taylor of Aldridge Volvo F88.
Vince Cooke Collection

These Moss and Lovatt pictures belong to Nigel Edwards. The company started in 1926 during the general strike. Nigel's grandparents were running the local corn mill and helped the farmers by taking their milk to the dairies in their corn wagon. This picture shows Victor Moss with a new Thorneycroft. Early 1950s at Moss and Lovatt's yard.

A fleet line-up in the yard in the early 1980s.

Stanley Edwards with a new Commer, 1967. Taken in the yard, they'd just swapped all the milk churns off the old lorry ready for the next day.

One of the vehicles still running when we finished in 2011. Taken in 2009.

Nigel has this vehicle and is keeping it to take to the shows.

Peter Foden CBE, Managing Director of ERf from 1960 until his retirement. He passed away last year, and is seen being taken to his resting place on ERF No. 1, driven by Graeme Turner.

2012 *Photo John Heath*

Peter Foden (left) with Chris Smith of REVS with the REVS vehicle at Kelsall, 2011. *John Heath*

Ken Southerton deserves a mention. Ken was a skilled engineer who served his time at ERF. He started in 1946 on the saws in the cutting shed and ended up as Superintendent in the Repair Shop. He finished in the late 1960s and set up Commercial Repairs, Alsager with his partner Emyry Griffiths. Ken passed away in 2005. His son Andrew let me have this photo - Andrew and brother Paul have both followed in their father's engineering footsteps.

A Michelin ERF
*Heath/Smith
Collection*

The winter of 1990.
Andrew Rhead on the M6
northbound Corley
services. *Andrew Rhead*

These show the chaos further down the motorway. The arrow
shows Maurice Hill's tanker behind another Jones vehicle.
Taken from the other direction they are at the bottom of the
picture. They were stranded for 36 hours.
Maurice Hill Collection

When drivers get hitched...! When Martin 'Fat Lad' Harding married Nikki a convoy of 16 vehicles took him from Talke to the wedding venue at Hollington. Two more escorted the bride. Martin's dad, Johnny, drove Martin's Agribulk vehicle. The other drivers were: Chris Harry, Martin Bennett, Steve Kirkham, Paul Noble, Duncan Ball, Sam Mace, Rob Forrester, Pete Price, Matthew Jones, Martin Shaw, James Clarke, Lee Worsey, James Joyce. Darren Potts, Richard Cleaver, Mark Jones, Craig Evans. 12 May 2012.

All photos on this page David Humphries

Vince Cooke's outfit on the ferry from Portsmouth to Le Havre in 1980. Now retired, Vince celebrates his 80th birthday this year. *Vince Cooke*

And.... Me
Thanks for reading the book

Thanks to Arthur Shirley and Pete Stevenson.

John Heath photo

For the two Davids

ACKNOWLEDGEMENTS

Thanks to all who've taken the time to share their stories and photos. Thanks also to John Heath, Carl Johnson, John Willmore, John Cooke (Potteries Omnibus Preservation Society), Vince and Jerry Cooke, Ian Taylor, Roger Forrester, Les Slymn, Les Bailey and Derek Hambleton for their help.

Back Cover
Top: A line-up of Mountford Bros Bedfords at a carnival, probably Bucknall c1950s. *John Breed Collection*
Middle: The first vehicle Arthur Shirley drove after passing his test at 17 - a 1950 Bedford O type.
Arthur (left) with brother, James at the depot. 2012. *John Heath*
Bottom: Bill Taylor's AEC 8-wheel bulk tipper outside the family home in Herbert St, Aldridge.
L-R: Pat Jones, Barbara & Elaine Taylor (Bill's daughters), cousin Hazel. c1951.